MORGAN COUNTY PUBLIC LIBRARY
110 SOUTH JEFFERSON STREET
MARTINSVILLE, IN 46151

W9-BRT-023

J   Siwanowicz, Igor.
590
SIW   Animals up close.

WITHDRAWN

Animals Up Close

Zoom in on the world's most incredible creatures

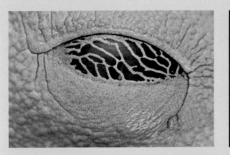
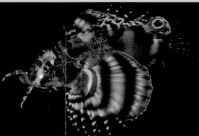

DK

LONDON, NEW YORK, MUNICH,
MELBOURNE, AND DELHI

Senior editor Amy-Jane Beer
Senior art editor Liz Sephton
Art editors Edward Kinsey, Chloe Luxford
Managing editor Camilla Hallinan
Managing art editor Owen Peyton Jones
Art director Martin Wilson
Associate publisher Andrew Macintyre
Category publisher Laura Buller
DK picture library Lucy Claxton, Rob Nunn
Illustration Peter Bull
Cartography Iorwerth Watkins
Creative techncal support Peter Pawsey
Senior production editor Vivianne Ridgeway
Senior production controller Pip Tinsley

First published in the United States in 2009 by
DK Publishing, 375 Hudson Street, New York, New York 10014

09 10 11 12 13 10 9 8 7 6 5 4 3 2
AD420 – 01/09

Photographs copyright © 2009 Igor Siwanowicz
Text copyright © 2009 Dorling Kindersley Limited

All rights reserved under International and Pan-American
Copyright Conventions. No part of this publication may be reproduced,
stored in a retrieval system, or transmitted in any form or by any means,
electronic, mechanical, photocopying, recording, or otherwise,
without the prior written permission of the copyright owner.
Published in Great Britain by Dorling Kindersley Limited.

A catalog record for this book is
available from the Library of Congress.

ISBN 978-0-7566-4513-7

Printed by Star Standard, Singapore

Discover more at
www.dk.com

Animals Up Close

Zoom in on the world's most incredible creatures

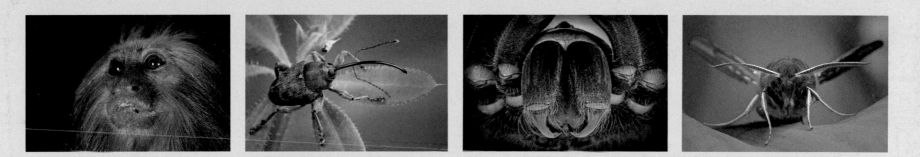

by Igor Siwanowicz

DK Publishing

Foreword

The animals in this book are small
enough to hold in your hands—often so
small they are easily overlooked. I've been
into bugs and other minibeasts since
before I could walk. My camera takes me
into hidden realms inhabited by all
kinds of exquisite, intricate, and bizarre
life forms. When you get up really
close, many of these creatures look
like aliens from another planet, but
their extraordinary shapes and features
are simply nature's solutions to the
everyday challenges of life in miniature. I try
to photograph animals from their own
perspective, which might mean getting down on my
hands and knees in the dirt! By getting up close, I hope to
show you how much personality they have, and why they
deserve to be admired, respected, and protected.

Igor Siwanowicz

Contents

P. S., look for the handy statistics about the animals starring in this book.
Distribution: maps show each species' native range, or where the animal occurs in the wild.
Status: conservation rankings are loosely based on the IUCN's Red List of threatened species.
Name: every species has a unique, two-part scientific name in Latin—the first part indicates its genus, or group of closely related organisms to which the animal belongs.
Life span: the normal life expectancy in the wild for a healthy animal lucky enough to reach old age.
Size: the average dimensions, as marked on the drawing—for example, length, height, or wingspan.

Life in miniature

For the small animals in this book, the world is a very different place from the one we experience. To a tiny frog or water bug, water is thick like syrup, with a springy surface like the film on pudding. To a female bird choosing a mate, the feathers of males reflect ultraviolet colors invisible to humans. To a hungry bat, the sound of a caterpillar chewing a leaf rings as loud and clear as a dinner bell. Despite these differences, the basic needs that drive all these creatures to feed, shelter, and reproduce are familiar to us, and with imagination we can put ourselves in their place.

This tree frog is close to the smallest possible size for a vertebrate (backboned) animal.

The bill can reach nectar produced deep inside tubular flowers.

Small problems

Small size presents certain physical problems. Small bodies have relatively large surfaces through which energy is lost in the form of heat. Weight for weight, small animals burn a lot more energy than large ones. Species such as this hummingbird survive by specializing in a high-energy diet. Others, such as the seahorse on page 44, adopt a low-energy lifestyle. Small animals also lose moisture through their large surface, so lifestyles that help conserve water are common. This is one reason why we often find small animals under stones, in burrows, in tree holes, and in other damp places.

The plant offers sweet nectar, rich in sugars, which gives the bird quick-release energy for its fast and furious lifestyle.

The hummingbird's wings beat more than 50 times a second as it hovers, burning energy at an enormous rate.

The challenge of life on Earth

The great biologist Charles Darwin realized that the unbelievable diversity of life we see on Earth is the result of a process he called natural selection, or survival of the fittest. He figured out that tiny differences between individuals could make a difference to their success in reproducing and passing on their special characteristics. Each of the beetles on the left is adapted to a very specific habitat and way of life, known as a niche. The 350,000 or so described species of beetle account for roughly a quarter of all known species.

Hidden talents

Small animals are naturally vulnerable to being eaten, but most have developed some kind of defense strategy. Some, such as this fish called a blenny, are masters of disguise. Others grow physical defenses such as spines or a tough shell. Some are toxic, and others pretend to be poisonous by mimicking warning colors. For some, sheer abundance is a survival tactic—by reproducing in vast numbers they improve the chances that some of their offspring will survive.

Eat or be eaten

Small does not necessarily mean helpless, and many of the animals you'll see in this book, like the Green jumping spider above, are fierce predators (hunters). Small animals catch their prey (victims) by giving chase, by ambush (lying in wait), or by setting ingenious traps such as silken webs. Their small but lethal weapons are used in stabbing, slicing, crushing, injecting poison, and other deadly techniques.

The woodlouse's body armor is made of a tough compound called chitin.

Mixed blessing

Many of the animals in this book have body designs that work extremely well on a small scale, but which also limit the size of the species. Land-dwelling woodlice like the one on the left rarely grow more than about 1¼ in (3 cm) long. The weight of body armor is one limiting factor—very large armored invertebrates, such as giant crabs, live only in the sea where the water helps support them. Animals that lack an efficient circulation system to deliver oxygen to their cells are also restricted in size—this is one reason you will never see an insect more than a few inches long. But within these limits, small animals show mind-blowing diversity, as we shall see.

The shapes of life

Animals are many-celled organisms that survive by feeding on plants or on other animals. They sense their environment and respond to it by moving around. In the half billion (500 million) years since animal life appeared on Earth, they have evolved (developed) an extraordinary variety of forms to help them perform these activities.

INVERTEBRATES

The animals we know as invertebrates all lack a backbone. They are often lumped together for convenience, but, in fact, they belong to about 30 very different groups, or phyla. Each phylum has distinct characteristics that set it apart from the others. Five of the largest and best known invertebrate phyla are described below.

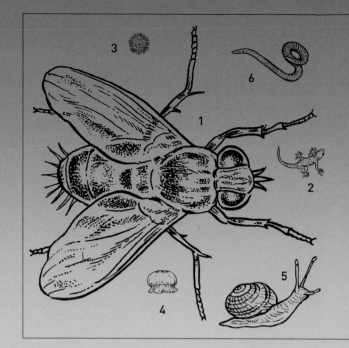

Cnidarians (phylum Cnidaria)
This group of simple animals includes corals, jellyfish, and sea anemones (above). All are armed with stinging cells, known as cnidocytes. Most of the 9,000 known species of cnidarian live in the sea, a few in fresh water.

Segmented worms (phylum Annelida)
This important group of about 15,000 species includes the familiar earthworms (above) as well as the leeches and many marine species such as tube worms, ragworms, and fanworms. The annelid body is made up of repeating segments.

Mollusks (phylum Mollusca)
This huge group of over 90,000 known species includes slugs, snails (above), and clams as well as the largest living invertebrate, the Colossal squid. Mollusks have a soft muscular body, protected in some by one or more shells. They live on land, in fresh water, and in the sea.

Echinoderms (phylum Echinodermata)
The name echinoderm means "spiny skin," and the 5,000 or so members of this group include starfish, sea urchins, and brittlestars (above). They live in the sea, and in some areas they are by far the most common living things.

Arthropods (phylum Arthropoda)
This is the largest and most diverse group of invertebrates on Earth. With over 1.2 million species already described, they make up more than four-fifths of all the known animal species. The word arthropod means "jointed leg" and the adults of all species have legs or other appendages that are supported by a suit of jointed body armor called an exoskeleton. The insects (above center), make up the largest arthropod group, followed by the arachnids (scorpions and spiders, above right), the crustaceans (crabs, shrimps, and woodlice), and the myriapods (centipedes and millipedes).

Diversity and abundance

The size of the animals illustrated on the left relates to the number of species in the major group, or phylum, to which they belong. The huge fly represents the staggering diversity of arthropods, of which there are about 1.2 million known species and perhaps millions more to be discovered. The total diversity of animal life on Earth may be as high as 10 million species. About 23 other animal phyla contain less familiar animals, none of which feature in this book.

1. Arthropods
2. Chordates
3. Echinoderms
4. Cnidarians
5. Mollusks
6. Annelids

CHORDATES

The chordate make up a large and important phylum of animals. A chordate's body is at some point in life supported by a stiffening rod called the notochord. Most chordates are also vertebrates. In vertebrates, the notochord is replaced early in development by a backbone made of small units (vertebrae) that link to provide support and flexibility and to protect the body's main nerve cord, which runs inside.

Notochord

The first chordates probably looked something like this lancelet, or amphioxus.

Power and precision

Having an internal skeleton with a stiff vertebral column not only helps vertebrate animals support their bodies, but the skeleton also gives muscles something to pull against. With the controlling influence of a brain, the skeleton and muscles of vertebrate animals allow them to perform a vast range of movements that require not only strength but also great precision and coordination.

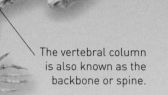

The vertebral column is also known as the backbone or spine.

Internal skeleton of a monitor lizard

The vertebrate body

All vertebrates have a head at one end and differ from most invertebrates in having an internal skeleton, including a skull. The skeleton is made of cartilage or bone. The body is bilaterally symmetrical (the same on both sides), with limbs and muscle groups arranged in pairs on either side of the vertebral column.

Fish

The first vertebrates were fish. They belong to several classes, one of which included the ancestor of all the other vertebrates, collectively known as tetrapods. Fish live in water and breathe using gills. Most lay eggs, but some bear live young.

Amphibians (class Amphibia)

Amphibians develop from aquatic (water-dwelling) young called tadpoles into air-breathing adults. Most have four legs as adults, and all must return to water to breed. They include frogs (above), toads, salamanders, and newts.

Reptiles (class Reptilia)

The reptiles are air-breathing animals with scaly, waterproof skin. They can live and breed on land, by laying eggs or bearing live young. Modern reptiles are ectothermic, meaning their bodies are not always warm, but they warm up with their surroundings.

Birds (class Aves)

The birds are descended directly from the reptiles. They have feathers, and they are warm-blooded (their body is always warm). The front limbs are modified into wings, used for flapping flight, though some have lost this ability. Young birds hatch from eggs.

Mammals (class Mammalia)

Mammals are warm-blooded air-breathers, and usually covered with fur or hair. Females feed young on milk from mammary glands. Mammal groups include rodents (rats and mice, above), cetaceans (whales and dolphins), and primates (monkeys, apes, and humans).

Into the wild

The best place to learn about the astounding diversity of life is in the wild. But when it comes to taking pictures of small animals, it helps me to have a specially built studio in which I can focus on composition, light, and form, with no distractions. In my home studio I can spend as long as I like creating each shot and setting everything exactly the way I want it. Photographing some of my favorite animals in their natural habitat was a completely different challenge, for which I had to travel to the other side of the world. I packed up my camera equipment and everything I thought I would need to create a portable studio in the jungle. Then I headed to West Papua, a remote part of Indonesia.

Passport to paradise
I spent three weeks in West Papua, on the island of New Guinea. It's one of the least explored regions on Earth, and not an easy place to get to. Natural obstacles such as mountains and dense jungle mean that the people here see very few visitors, and the habitats are among the most pristine in the world. It's a zoologist's paradise.

Friend or foe?
I met this fierce-looking Dani warrior on my first day in West Papua. I didn't want to annoy him by pointing my camera in his face, but I needn't have worried. The people here are as warm and friendly as anyone I've ever met. What's more, they love to pose.

Willing helpers
I would never have found all the amazing insects I wanted to see without the help of local children. Using a sketchbook and a few words of the local language, I was able to tell them which species I wanted, and they soon realized this was an easy way to earn candy!

My field studio

Choosing my equipment carefully meant that I was able to set up a simple studio in the middle of nowhere. As you can see, I was never short of assistants. The one holding the umbrella was essential. It seemed to rain every five minutes and a wet camera would have been disastrous.

Rubber air blower for removing dust particles from the camera lens

A "third hand" for holding twigs, sticks, and leaves

Extension tube for macro work

In the gear bag

I took two cameras and just two lenses, with fixed focal lengths of 24 and 100 mm. I also had a set of extension tubes for macro work and a remote cable shutter release. I took two flash guns with diffusers to soften the light, and two tripods, one for the camera and one for hanging backdrops. Finally, I had to pack about 5 lbs (2 kg) of batteries, 20 GB of memory cards, and a 40 GB portable hard drive.

Remote cable shutter release

Batteries for my flashes and the camera

Portable hard drive

Flash diffuser

Flash hot shoe and cable

Jungle challenges

Photography in the jungle is tricky. A scene looks different from every angle and it's never easy to move around. A slip or a trip can lead to a nasty fall—or worse, dropping precious equipment into the mud. The humidity makes it difficult to keep equipment dry and when it comes to photographing animals, the hardest part is finding them in the first place!

Flash

Greater of two weevils

Weevils are a type of beetle and are easy to recognize by their distinctive long rostrum, or snout. There are more than 60,000 species throughout the world, and they are mostly parasitic—each species lives inside and feeds on a specific plant, called its host. Many weevils are pests, infesting field crops and lumber plantations. The encounter presented in this picture could take place, at least in theory—these two species do both live in the same environment—but since they feed on different plants they are unlikely to cross paths in their natural habitat.

The weevil's head has a ball-and-socket joint, which allows it to swivel from side to side, giving the insect a wide field of vision.

The rostrum has small jaws at the tip, used for feeding. A female weevil also uses her jaws to bore holes into the wood, seeds, leaves, or roots of the food plant. Then she carefully places her eggs inside so that when the grubs hatch they can begin feeding right away.

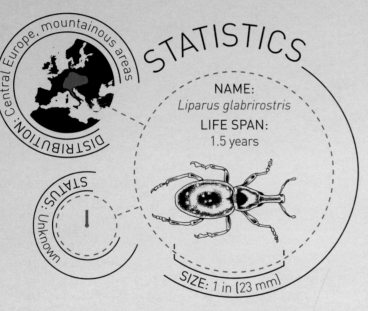

DISTRIBUTION: Central Europe, mountainous areas

STATISTICS

NAME:
Liparus glabrirostris

LIFE SPAN:
1.5 years

STATUS: Unknown

SIZE: 1 in (23 mm)

Greater weevil
Liparus glabrirostris is Europe's largest species of weevil, measuring up to 23 mm (1 in) long. It lives in mountainous regions, such as the Alps, which is where I found this particular individual. Its main food plants are butterbur and coltsfoot.

The weevil's antennae (feelers) are jointed. They can be folded and sheathed in special grooves running along the side of the rostrum to protect them.

Like other insects, weevils have compound eyes. The eyes are particularly sensitive to rapid movements that could signal danger, such as an attacking predator.

This weevil's mottled brown coloring provides excellent camouflage against the bark of its host plant.

Lesser weevil
This little weevil, *Pissodes pini*, is just ¼–½ in (6–8 mm) long and infests damaged or sickly pine trees. The female lays its eggs in holes she's made in the bark. When the larvae emerge, they create a network of tiny tunnels by eating their way through the wood.

The shiny black exoskeleton is tough and protects the weevil from many predators, including other beetles, birds, and lizards. However it may still fall victim to larger predators—it is big enough to make a crunchy but worthwhile snack for a fox or an owl.

The yellow markings are made of short, thick scales that look like hairs.

Parasites and farmers

Female weevils deposit eggs inside their host food plant. The newly hatched larvae, or grubs, feed on the inside of the host before pupating. The adult weevils emerge from the pupae and feed on the outside of the host plant. Occasionally, this kills the host and they have to move to another. Some weevils farm fungi inside the host plant. As the fungus develops inside specially created chambers, it breaks down the plant tissues, creating a nutritious mulch for the weevils to eat. Unfortunately, some fungi can be fatal to the host plant.

Some species of weevil have become flightless during their evolution. The elytra, or forewings, are fused together on the weevil's back.

The weevil's lower legs and feet are armed with sharp spikes, which help it to cling onto the leaves and stems of its food plant.

Slender loris

This gangly little primate was given its name by Dutch explorers. The word *loris* is Dutch for clown, and having watched this goggle-eyed character swaying around on his branch I can see why. His enormous eyes allow him to see well in the dark, but in order to focus clearly he needs to move his head back and forth. When he sees something puzzling (like a photographer and his equipment) he pauses and rocks gently to get a better look. The effect is both comical and endearing.

The eyes take up as much space in the skull as the brain. The huge pupils take in as much light as possible, allowing the loris to see even in very dim conditions. Light is detected by cells called photoreceptors in a part of the eye called the retina. A reflective layer at the back of the eye, called the *tapetum lucidum,* ensures that no light is wasted—it is all directed to the retina. The *tapetum lucidum* is what makes the eyes of many nocturnal animals shine in the dark.

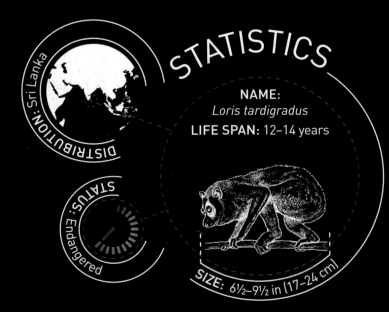

STATISTICS

DISTRIBUTION: Sri Lanka

NAME:
Loris tardigradus
LIFE SPAN: 12–14 years

STATUS: Endangered

SIZE: 6½–9½ in (17–24 cm)

The pink nose has a moist surface, the rhinarium, like that of a dog. Animals with moist noses tend to have a very acute sense of smell, with many thousands more scent receptors than dry-nosed species such as humans.

The loris has teeth well suited to its varied diet. Lorises eat fruit, insects, bird eggs, and gum. The teeth of the lower jaw stick out at an angle that allows the loris to scrape sap and gum from trees and to comb grease and grime from its fine fur.

Distant relatives

Lorises are primates, like us, but they sit on a rather distant branch of our family tree. They belong to a group known as the prosimians, or pre-monkeys, which also includes bushbabies, pottos, and tarsiers. All are nocturnal (active by night) and spend their whole lives in trees. They try to avoid competition with true monkeys, which are active mainly by day (diurnal).

The loris cleans its ears with a specially adapted claw on its second toe. Known as the toilet claw, because it is used for grooming and cleaning, it is much longer than the other claws, which are short and flat, like human finger and toenails.

The fur is thick and woolly but very fine. The dense coat is waterproof as long as its remains in good condition, so lorises spend a lot of time grooming.

Hold on tight

The loris has paws shaped for climbing. The thumbs and big toes are large and create a strong grasp, but lorises are not as nimble-fingered as monkeys or apes. Unlike many other primates, the loris has no tail to use for balance, so it climbs rather carefully, pausing often. As the name Slender loris suggests, the arms and legs are long and extremely slim, not much thicker than a pencil.

Variegated locust

It's no bigger than my thumb, but in many African farming communities, this colorful species of grasshopper is public enemy number one. Locusts are a problem because they occur in huge numbers. A swarm can destroy a whole crop in minutes. However, the locusts don't have it all their own way—in parts of Nigeria and Cameroon people collect them by the thousand, cook them, and eat them. Apparently the flavor varies depending on which plants the insects themselves have been feeding on.

STATISTICS

NAME:
Zonocerus variegatus

LIFE SPAN:
About 1 year

SIZE: 1½–2¼ in (35–55 mm)

DISTRIBUTION: Sub-Saharan Africa

STATUS: Pest / Not threatened

Warning colors

Adult locusts are weak, slow flyers. This makes them an easy target for predators, yet many animals avoid eating them. The dramatic colors are a warning that the locust is capable of producing a foul-tasting, even toxic, secretion. Not all locusts taste bad, only those that have been eating certain toxic plants. But any predator that tastes a bad one learns to associate the colors with a nasty experience and so even the non-foul-tasting locusts are protected.

Locusts have good eyesight, but unlike us they see the world as a mosaic of small images, formed by the hundreds of tiny lenses that make up each compound eye. Compound eyes are especially sensitive to movement, and locusts are able to detect danger approaching from almost any angle.

Locust plagues

Every 10 or 20 years, parts of Africa and Asia suffer locust plagues. The most recent was in 2004, when swarms of locusts caused national emergencies in several West African countries. A locust eats its own body weight in food each day. This is only about 0.07 oz (2 g), but locust swarms can be millions strong and can devastate a landscape in just a few hours.

The first pair of mouthparts are fused to form the labrum, or lip. This shields the more intricate mouthparts from damage as the locust barges its away around the food plant.

The mandibles (jaws) are powerful cutters, able to chop up even tough plant material.

Toxic shock
Toxic and foul-tasting chemicals are collected from the locust's gut and stored in a gland in the abdomen. The gland releases its content if the insect is attacked, providing a nasty shock the predator won't forget.

Touch and taste-sensitive, mobile mouthparts called palps help the locust manipulate its food and decide what is edible—for this species, that's almost anything.

Horned lizards in love

Sometimes misleadingly known as horned toads because of their unusual round body and broad head, these fascinating reptiles have always been among my favorite animals. Not only do they look like miniature armored dinosaurs, but they also have some amazing adaptations to life in the desert, and a truly unique method of self-defense.

Lines of defense
Although its stout, armored body makes it far from nimble, this little reptile is well-equipped for survival against a variety of predators, including hawks and coyotes. Its coloring provides camouflage, and when threatened, it puffs up its spiny body, becoming larger than life and almost impossible to swallow. It may also half bury itself in the sand to make it difficult for a predator to take hold. As a spectacular last resort, this lizard can burst the tiny blood vessels around its eyes and shoot foul-tasting blood at an aggressor up to 3 ft (1 m) away.

Water, water!
The lizard's skin is covered in tiny grooves that direct water from all over its body toward its mouth. This means it can gain moisture even by walking on dew that has condensed on rocks and sand. When it rains, the lizard lifts its tail and the scales on its back to create a gutter that channels water forward and downward to its head.

The eyes are shielded against direct sunlight by horny brows, and thick eyelids protect against the bites of angry ants.

Courtship
Horned lizards take part in a brief courtship before mating in spring. The female lays about a dozen eggs in a burrow—they develop and hatch alone.

The lizards often sunbathe with only their head poking out of the sand. The outline of the head is disguised by the spiky horns, and a special arrangement of blood vessels carries heat from the head to warm the whole body.

The lizard has a sticky tongue, which it uses to scoop up mouthfuls of tiny insects, especially ants, for food.

STATISTICS

DISTRIBUTION: Southern US, northern Mexico

NAME:
Phrynosoma platyrhinos
LIFE SPAN: 8 years

STATUS: Low risk

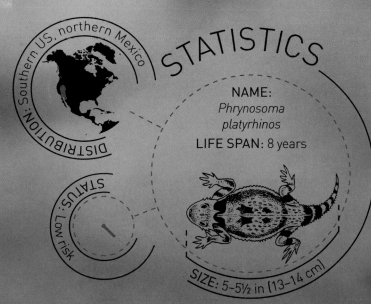

SIZE: 5–5½ in (13–14 cm)

Sea urchin

The skeletons of sea urchins make wonderful beachcombing souvenirs. They have a beautiful pattern of radiating dots (the tubercles where the spines were attached), holes (pores where tube feet once emerged) and zigzag fissures (the joins between plates in the skeleton). The living animal is just as lovely, and surprisingly lively, too, with its colorful spines bristling and tube feet waving in the water.

If I only had a brain...
Sea urchins and their relatives (including starfish and sea cucumbers) have no brain. They manage to achieve all the processes required to survive with a simple arrangement of five main nerve cords radiating out from a ring surrounding the mouth.

Each spine is attached by a ball-and-socket joint that allows it to be raised and lowered or swiveled to provide maximum protection or help wedge the urchin in a rocky crevice.

The urchin has hundreds of tube feet that it operates hydraulically (with water pressure). Each ends in a small sucker. The urchin uses its tube feet for creeping, collecting food and camouflage materials, securing itself to the seabed, sensing chemicals, and extracting oxygen from the water.

The mouth is in the middle of the urchin's underside. It contains five chalky teeth that scrape up morsels of food including algae and the remains of animals. The tips of two teeth are just visible here.

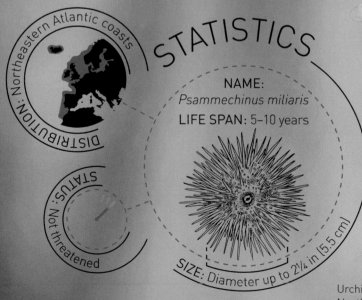

STATISTICS

DISTRIBUTION: Northeastern Atlantic coasts

NAME:
Psammechinus miliaris
LIFE SPAN: 5–10 years

STATUS: Not threatened

SIZE: Diameter up to 2¼ in (5.5 cm)

Young drifters
Like many relatively slow-moving, bottom-dwelling marine animals, sea urchins have drifting larvae. Urchin larvae are only about 0.08 in (2 mm) long, but can drift hundreds of miles in ocean currents. This disperses each urchin's offspring far and wide.

Urchins are far from defenseless. Nestling among their spines are many tiny organs called pedicellariae. These consist of three-way pincers mounted on a mobile stalk. The urchin uses them to pick off encrusting algae and unwanted passengers. Some pedicellariae can also deliver a sting.

Scorpion mother

Scorpions are an ancient group of arachnids that have been in existence for over 400 million years. Closely related to spiders, they are often greatly feared for their venom. In fact, most scorpions are timid and shy, and rarely use their sting. This species hails from the Mediterranean region and lives in dry woodland, under stones, logs, and piles of bark. I found this devoted mother lurking in just such a spot, with her precious brood jostling for position on her back.

Sting in the tail

The venom in a scorpion's sting consists of small proteins that disrupt the normal function of the victim's nervous system, paralyzing it and often killing it outright. It is especially effective against spiders and insects. To humans, the sting of *Euscorpius* is no more serious than a mosquito bite, though some people can suffer a severe allergic reaction. The venom is generally only used in self defense, or when the scorpion cannot subdue prey by using its claws alone.

All aboard

Unlike female spiders, a female scorpion gives birth to live young after performing a complex mating ritual with a male. She carries her babies around on her back for safety, until they have molted, or shed their exoskeleton, for the first time—with a tougher new exoskeleton, they are less vulnerable. The male scorpion plays no part in the care of his offspring.

Glow-in-the-dark

Scorpion armor contains a fluorescent protein that glows faintly in the dark and radiates brightly under an ultraviolet light. Scorpions are mostly nocturnal so it's possible the fluorescence helps them to see one another at night.

The sting at the end of the tail is made up of a pair of swollen venom glands and a spine that acts like a hypodermic needle to inject the poison.

The young are paler than their parents. The new exoskeleton that appears after each molt is tougher and darker than the one before, offering improved protection at every stage.

Young scorpions will molt up to seven times before reaching maturity.

The scorpion's body is covered in tiny sensory hairs that detect vibrations in the ground caused by prey walking or burrowing nearby.

A scorpion with small, slender claws is likely to be more venomous than one with large, powerful claws.

The scorpion's mouthparts are more like small claws than jaws. Known as chelicerae, the scorpion uses them to crush and tear food into small pieces. The fragments of food are dissolved by potent digestive chemicals in the mouth, and the scorpion devours the resulting nutritious soup—no chewing required.

STATISTICS

NAME:
Euscorpius sicanus

LIFE SPAN: 3–4 years

SIZE: 3/4–1¼ in (2–3 cm)

DISTRIBUTION: Mediterranean

STATUS: Unknown

The strong pedipalps (claws) are used to grab and pin down prey, and may also be used to begin the task of dismembering it for consumption.

Rascally Rainbow lorikeet

Rainbow lorikeets are familiar birds in parts of Australia, Indonesia, and the South Pacific. Their glorious colors and extrovert personality make them popular as pets and with tourists, who enjoy the acrobatic and clownish antics the birds perform, seemingly just for fun. Unfortunately, their feeding and bathroom habits can mean disaster for fruit farmers.

Glowing colors

The harlequin colors of the lorikeet's plumage are produced by just four pigments: lutein (yellow), astaxantin (red), pheomelanin (brown), and eumelanin (black). The dazzling blue of the head and throat feathers is a structural color, produced not by pigment, but by the arrangement of microscopic barbs on the feathers, which absorb red wavelengths of light and reflect only blue.

Like other parrots, lorikeets are smart. Parrot brains are unusually large in bird terms—in fact, size for size, they're almost as big as primate brains.

Feeding habits

The sharp beak is used for opening seeds, but also comes in handy for self defense. Birds have no teeth, so solid foods are ground up in a muscular part of the digestive system called the gizzard—the lorikeet sometimes swallows grit to help the grinding process along. The lorikeet's tongue looks like a brush, with lots of tiny bristles that help mop up liquid foods like nectar, sap, and fruit juices. The scientific name *Trichoglossus* means "hairy tongue".

Most parrots have excellent eyesight, and the lorikeet is no exception. Full color vision allows them to spot ripe fruits, and recognize other birds at a distance.

Fruity feast

Lorikeets love fruit. They also eat seeds and nuts, which they skillfully prize open with their powerful beak. Unfortunately, they often destroy crops well before the fruit has a chance to ripen and be harvested, and they damage other trees by eating the buds. What they don't eat is often ruined anyway with a splattering of sloppy droppings.

He or she?

Unlike the Gouldian finch on page 70, in which the sexes look very different, male and female Rainbow lorikeets are almost impossible to tell apart just by looking. Only they know the difference.

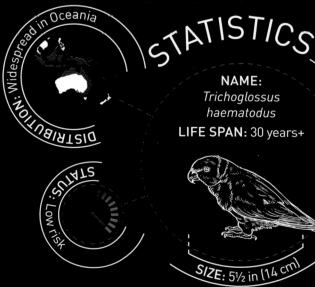

DISTRIBUTION: Widespread in Oceania

STATISTICS

STATUS: Low risk

NAME:
*Trichoglossus
haematodus*
LIFE SPAN: 30 years+

SIZE: 5½ in (14 cm)

Giant silkmoth caterpillar

NAME:
Eupackardia calleta

LARVAL LIFE SPAN:
About 5 weeks

SIZE: 4 in (10 cm)

DISTRIBUTION: Southern US & Central America

STATUS: Not threatened

The family of giant silkmoths includes some of the largest moths in existence. The adult of this North American species, the Calleta silkmoth, has a wingspan of up to 4¾ in (12 cm), and its funky-looking caterpillar grows about as long as my index finger.

The colorful nodules and spines that give the mature caterpillar its eccentric appearance are not just about decoration. Their festive colors are a warning to all that the caterpillar is toxic.

Cycle of life

Emerging from eggs as tiny black larvae, these caterpillars grow rapidly. They molt (shed their skin) five times, becoming increasingly colorful on each occasion, before beginning pupation—the final stage in their development. The adult moths do not feed, relying instead on the fat stored by the caterpillar. They live only for a week or so after emerging from the pupa—just enough time to mate and lay eggs that will become the next batch of caterpillars.

The caterpillar eats almost constantly. The powerful jaw muscles, which make short work of leafy material, virtually fill the head. The microscopic brain takes up hardly any space at all.

There are six tiny eyelets, or stemmata, just out of sight on each side of the lower part of the head. These can probably detect light and dark, but not color or shape.

Pupation
It's difficult to see what goes on inside a silkmoth cocoon, but other species use silk only to secure themselves while they pupate. The pictures above show a swallowtail butterfly caterpillar (whose colors indicate that it too is toxic), attaching to a stem, then transforming into a pupa.

The caterpillar's crawling feet, or prolegs, are equipped with rows of grasping hooks known as crochets.

This small round opening is a spiracle, or breathing hole. There's one on each side of every segment of the caterpillar's body.

Silk spinners
After completing its fifth molt the caterpillar begins spinning silk from a gland in its tail end. It creates a covering called a cocoon within which it forms a pupa and metamorphoses (transforms) into the adult moth you see over the page. In silk farms, the cocoons are collected and the silk is spun again to produce thread for making fine fabrics.

The thorny nodules covering the body of the mature caterpillar are packed with toxins. If the nodule is touched, the toxin oozes out from around the base of each spine.

The caterpillar's soft, segmented body contains around 4,000 muscles. We humans have a mere 629 muscles.

Getting a leg up
Caterpillars have two kinds of legs—true legs and prolegs. The small true legs near the front of the caterpillar's body later become the legs of the adult moth. The caterpillar uses them to hold food. The prolegs, near the back, help the caterpillar move about, but they disappear during metamorphosis (transformation) into an adult moth.

Superhero silkmoth

I discovered this marvelous creature one morning in the hatchery where I keep moth pupae. It was a bit of surprise, since the caterpillar (the one you see on the previous page) had only spun its silken cocoon about three months earlier, and this species can often spend two years or more as a pupa. In this pose, waiting for his wings to harden, I think this male looks a little like a mysterious action hero, with a sinister dark mask and velvety black cape.

These enormous antennae are covered in minute chemical sensors called olfactory sensilla. They are so sensitive they can detect single molecules of special scents (pheromones) given off by female moths when they are ready to mate. Using this super-sense the male can home in on a female from over a mile away.

Powered flight

The Calleta silkmoth is one of the world's largest insect species. Its close relative, the Atlas moth, has the largest wings of any insect—each wing is the size of a human hand. Not surprisingly, silkmoths are powerful flyers, able to make journeys of several miles a night in search of mating opportunities.

Eyesight is of secondary importance in an insect that is guided mostly by its sense of smell. However, the moth will respond to bright lights, avoiding them by day in an effort to hide from visual predators but often flying erratically toward them at night.

The upper surfaces of the wings appear uniformly dark at first glance, but closer inspection shows them to be exquisitely decorated with spots, arcs, and a lacelike tracery of veins in violet, lavender, and brown.

As a caterpillar, this moth did little but eat. As an adult it will not feed at all. The mouthparts wasted away during the moth's time in the pupa and it must now rely solely on stored fat reserves to see it through its 10-day-long adult life.

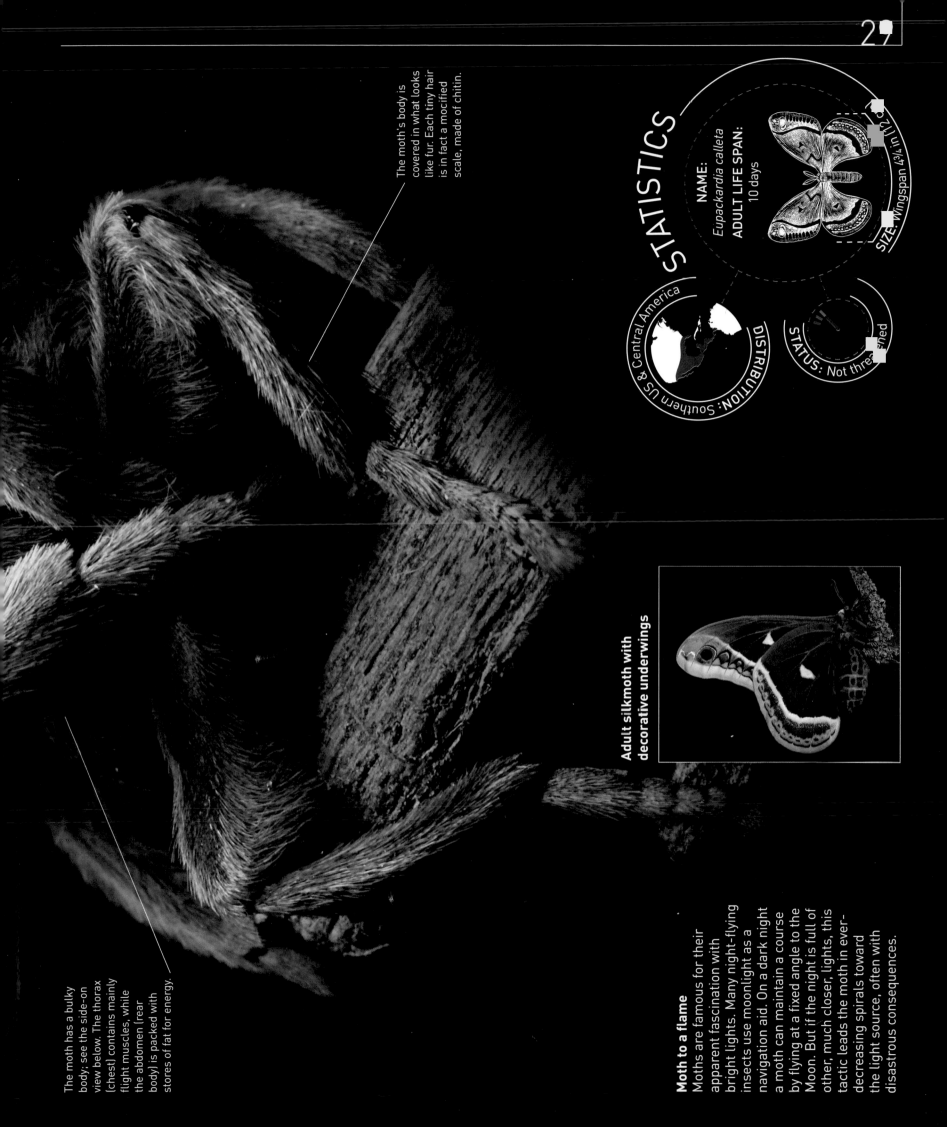

The moth's body is covered in what looks like fur. Each tiny hair is in fact a modified scale, made of chitin.

STATISTICS

NAME:
Eupackardia calleta
ADULT LIFE SPAN:
10 days

SIZE: Wingspan 4¾ in (12 c

DISTRIBUTION: Southern US & Central America

STATUS: Not threatened

The moth has a bulky body; see the side-on view below. The thorax (chest) contains mainly flight muscles, while the abdomen (rear body) is packed with stores of fat for energy.

Adult silkmoth with decorative underwings

Moth to a flame

Moths are famous for their apparent fascination with bright lights. Many night-flying insects use moonlight as a navigation aid. On a dark night a moth can maintain a course by flying at a fixed angle to the Moon. But if the night is full of other, much closer, lights, this tactic leads the moth in ever-decreasing spirals toward the light source, often with disastrous consequences.

Ageless axolotl

The axolotl is an amazing amphibian that seems to have discovered the secret of eternal youth. It spends its whole life in water and keeps the frilly external gills that its salamander relatives lose when they crawl on to dry land to begin adult life. This neat trick of delaying adulthood is known as neoteny, and it has always fascinated zoologists.

If the axolotl loses a limb, a gill, or even its whole tail, it can regrow it almost as good as new. The renewal process can take several months, but waiting is much better than losing the body part forever.

Each feathery gill is made up of a central stem, the rachis, and many ultra-fine fronds, called fimbriae. The skin covering each gill is so thin that oxygen dissolved in the water is able to pass directly into the axolotl's bloodstream.

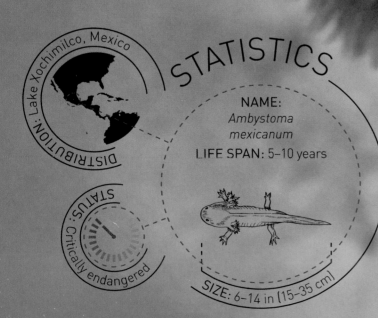

DISTRIBUTION: Lake Xochimilco, Mexico

STATISTICS

NAME:
Ambystoma mexicanum
LIFE SPAN: 5–10 years

STATUS: Critically endangered

SIZE: 6–14 in (15–35 cm)

The skin is very soft and thin, and under normal circumstances never develops the waxy waterproofing seen on other adult salamanders.

Forever young

While the axolotl keeps the external appearance of a tadpole all its life, its reproductive organs still mature in the normal way, and it is able to breed in its juvenile form. Experiments in laboratories have shown that all an axolotl needs to develop into an adult salamander is a dose of iodine, which encourages it to produce natural chemicals called growth hormones. But in the wild, axolotls are much better off staying in the water and rearing their young there.

The eyes have iridescent irises and in this albino individual, a bright red pupil.

Almost gone

Sadly, there is now only one place where axolotls survive in the wild, an area of wetland in central Mexico. Other populations became extinct when the lakes where they lived dried up or became polluted. Being unable to travel over land means axolotls cannot escape poor conditions, so if their last wetland deteriotates, axolotls will become extinct.

A choice of colors

Axolotls come in many genetic color varieties. These include the traditional wild type, which is brown, gray, or black with dark spots; albino (golden with pink eyes); leucistic (white with black eyes); melanoid (very dark with no iridescence); and axanthic (lacking iridescent and yellow pigment). Specimens can be bred with a combination of these, such as white albino (white with pink eyes), or melanoid albino (white with almost invisible yellow spots and no shiny pigment).

The axolotl's mouth is so big that when it opens suddenly, the inrush of water carries any prey unlucky enough to be close by straight in. It's a neat hunting technique that uses very little energy.

Mongolian gerbil

Best known as a loveable pet, this charismatic animal is also called a jird. Gerbils are rodents—relatives of squirrels, mice, and hamsters. They live wild in the dry, stony deserts of Asia. Gerbils are highly inquisitive, industrious creatures, with patterns of activity that compare best with those of a college student—up at all hours of the day or night, then crashing out for a few hours' sleep at irregular intervals.

Pet subject

Gerbils make very good pets. Unlike hamsters, they are active during the daytime when their owners are awake. They produce very little urine and their droppings are dry, easy to clean up, and do not smell. Given plenty of dry bedding material such as hay or paper (they make wonderful document shredders) pet gerbils will construct intricate mazes of tunnels in their cage.

Family ties

Gerbils live in complex burrow systems, often in family groups. Because brothers and sisters often continue to live together as adults, in many family groups the male helping rear the young is not their father, but their uncle. This is a very unusual arrangement, but makes sense in terms of evolution because the males are still looking after young to which they are genetically related.

The insulation provided by the gerbil's slightly shaggy fur works both ways. At night it helps conserve heat and by day it protects the gerbil's skin from the fierce rays of the sun.

Long whiskers serve the gerbil well in the gloom of its burrow, and help it feel its way at night. The hair cell, or follicle, from which each whisker sprouts is connected directly to the gerbil's nervous system. The whiskers are so important that baby gerbils are born with them, even though they have no other hair.

The back legs are much longer and more powerful than those at the front. The gerbil is able to leap away from danger and hop at great speed, looking a bit like a tiny kangaroo.

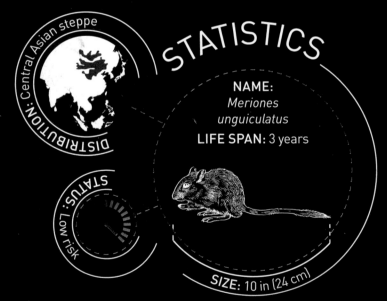

DISTRIBUTION: Central Asian steppe

STATISTICS

NAME:
Meriones unguiculatus
LIFE SPAN: 3 years

STATUS: Low risk

SIZE: 10 in (24 cm)

Gerbils have sensitive hearing. The prominent ears are furry to protect them from heat and cold, and able to twitch forward and back in order to focus on faint sounds.

The eyes bulge to the sides of the head, allowing the gerbil a very wide field of view. This is a sure sign of an animal more used to being hunted than hunting.

Dry rations

Gerbils are experts in desert survival. They remain active all year round, and plan ahead for hard times by collecting spare seeds and grains and storing them in dry pantry chambers in their burrow. They hardly ever drink and manage to acquire all the moisture they need to survive from their food and by licking up dew.

The gerbil's tail is as long as the rest of its body. It serves as a counterbalance when the gerbil hops quickly, and can be flicked from side to side to help with fast cornering. Its dark tip is thought to act as a decoy, directing the attention of predators away from the owner's head and body.

Gerbils have sharp, stout claws, ideal for digging in the coarse desert soil. The paws are dexterous enough to sort seeds from sand with ease.

Hungry centipede

The word *centipede* comes from Latin, meaning one hundred legs. Centipedes can have anything up to 382 legs, but ironically the total leg-count is never exactly 100, because there is always an odd number of leg-bearing body segments. The closest any centipede can get to 100 legs is 98 or 102, though for most familiar species the average is less than 50. To other small invertebrates, however, what matters about centipedes is not the exact number of legs, but the huge poison-pumping fangs. All centipedes are voracious predators.

Fancy footwork
With so many legs to organize, walking requires careful coordination if the centipede is to avoid trips and tangles. The most important factor is timing. Each leg moves in strict order, immediately following the one in front, like a Mexican wave.

STATISTICS

NAME:
Scolopendra cingulata

LIFE SPAN: 5–10 years

DISTRIBUTION: Mediterranean

SIZE: 4–5½ in (10–14 cm)

STATUS: Not threatened

Centipedes have one pair of legs per body segment. In a millipede, there appear to be two pairs of legs per segment because the segments are fused together in pairs.

The maxillipeds sprout from the first body segment and form fangs. The tip of each fang is connected to a poison gland.

Many centipedes are blind, but this species has two clusters of light-sensitive ommatidia forming primitive compound eyes.

The centipede's heart is a tube that runs the length of the body, pulsing rhythmically. In this picture you can make it out as a dark line down the middle of some segments.

The antennae provide the centipede with most of its sensory input. They help it feel its way and locate food. Potential prey will be recognized and seized the instant an antenna makes contact.

Dark deeds

The rudimentary eyes of the banded centipede are of little use for seeing—they are merely simple light sensors that help the centipede avoid brightly lit places where it might be spotted by a larger predator. Acute vision would be wasted on an animal that lives almost exclusively in the dark. Instead, the centipede relies on its long antennae to hunt and find its way around at night. By day, it seeks out dark hiding places.

The centipede is an all-out carnivore, completely uninterested in the vegetable matter that formed its vegetarian victim's last meal. The greens are ignored as the centipede tucks in.

Dinner today is a Migratory locust, but centipedes eat all kinds of other invertebrate animals. They will also eat carrion (dead animals), and other rotting organic material, but they much prefer a fresh kill.

Burrowing owl

He has the intense glare and lethally sharp bill and talons (claws) of a fierce predator, but, in fact, this tiny owl would be dwarfed by a large rabbit. The scientific name *Athene* comes from the Greek goddess of wisdom, and owls appear all-knowing, with their penetrating stare. In reality, they have a fairly small brain, but this would be of little comfort to the Burrowing owl's victims. This miniature hunter tracks its prey with just as much ferocity and precision as hawks, eagles, and other owls many times its size.

Sociable owl
While many owls live alone most of the time, Burrowing owls seem to like company. In areas of very good habitat such as fertile prairie, there may be dozens of owls sharing the same extensive burrow system, to which they may continue adding new tunnels, entrances, and chambers over time.

The owl's mottled plumage (feathers) provides excellent camouflage as it moves around on the ground, blending well with dry stony landscapes and scrubby vegetation.

For a bird that spends much of its time on the ground, the Burrowing owl is a remarkable flier. Unusually for an owl, it is able to hover, and can beat each wing independently of the other, a skill that adds greatly to its mid-air maneuverability.

The legs are long and strong, making the owl an excellent runner and digger. As its name suggests, the owl is able to excavate its own burrow, though often it prefers simply to move in to one dug by another animal.

STATISTICS

DISTRIBUTION: North, Central, & South America

STATUS: Low risk

NAME:
Athene cunicularia
LIFE SPAN: 9 years

SIZE: Height 8-11 in (20-28 cm)

The owl's neck contains twice as many vertebrae as ours, allowing the head to rotate through about 270 degrees.

The owl has acute vision, even in low-light levels, thanks to a reflective layer at the back of the eye that directs light onto the retina. Unlike most owls, the Burrowing owl sees in color. The tubular shape of owl eyeballs means they can't roll in their sockets—hence the need for a very flexible neck.

The distinctive shape of the owl's face is formed by the arrangement of feathers, which help funnel sound toward the ears, hidden just behind the eyes.

The bill is pointed and sharply hooked. Prey is killed with a precision bite to the neck.

Beetle mania

In addition to small mammals, frogs, and lizards, Burrowing owls eat a lot of insects. They sometimes collect the droppings of mammals and scatter them in and around their burrow. The dung attracts beetles, which then make easy pickings for the owl.

Mantis strikes a pose

Like an alien on the attack, the Giant devil's flower mantis possesses all the sinister beauty suggested by its exotic name. When threatened, it rears up to face its enemy, spreads its arms, and flashes a sudden, startling display of color. This species of mantis is by far my personal favorite and seems to love showing off for the camera! It originates from the hot, humid scrublands of subtropical Africa.

The forelegs bear dense arrays of spines and bristles, which help to snag and grip the bodies of flying insect prey.

This is a pose calculated to startle would-be predators that get too close, such as birds and perhaps even small monkeys. When the mantis raises its front legs, it seems to double in size. The petal-like flanges (outgrowths) on the legs are turned forward, maximizing their apparent size and the dramatic effect of the brilliant colors. Combined with an apparently penetrating glare, the overall impression is somewhat menacing. But at less than 4 in (10 cm) long the mantis is no real threat to anything other than the flying insects on which it feeds.

The shape and color of the legs bear a striking resemblance to the petals of the insect's plant namesake, the devil's flower.

Antennae help the mantis to smell by catching scents carried in the air. Being a male, this individual has feathery antennae—those of females are straight.

The dark spots on the eyes are called pseudopupils. They give the impression the mantis is staring right at you, but, in fact, they bear no relation to the direction the mantis is looking. In reality a mantis never focuses its gaze in just one direction at a time. Each of the hundreds of ommatidia making up the compound eyes points in a slightly different direction. The dark spots are the bases of the few ommatidia that face toward the observer.

The upper section of the mantis body is called the prothorax. It gives the mantis a degree of flexibility not seen in many insects, allowing it to bend and stretch to reach prey and to adopt this striking threat posture. The lower part of the body is much less flexible.

Standing out, blending in

Against a simple studio backdrop, the mantis appears almost gaudy. But in its native forest habitat, its bold coloration provides superb camouflage, making it all but invisible to predators and prey. Interestingly, the intensity of the colors varies depending on humidity (the amount of moisture in the air). Humidity affects the color of foliage (leaves), so the mantis changes, too, in order to maintain its disguise whatever the conditions. Some species have even been known to turn black to match the sooty branches of trees after a forest fire.

Growing pains

A mantis takes nearly a year to reach adulthood, and as it grows it molts (sheds) its exoskeleton 9 or 10 times. Females molt once more than males and grow bigger as a result. When it first emerges from an egg, the young mantis, or nymph, is black and glossy and looks like an ant. The early instars, or molting stages, are very bright, even white. Then their color becomes darker with each molt, and they resemble dead leaves. The gorgeous adult coloring finally appears about a week after the last molt.

Camouflage is so important for this species that it has even developed leaflike flaps to disguise its spindly legs.

The mantis breathes through tiny holes called spiracles, located around its body. Sometimes it will force air through them to make a threatening hissing sound to frighten off a predator.

Two sets of translucent wings drape from the mantis's thorax like the folds of a stiff cape. However, this species is no great aviator, and can only fly short distances, either to escape a predator or to find a new place to sit and wait for its prey. Males of smaller mantis species may fly considerable distances following the alluring scent of a female.

The rear legs, although very slender, are quite strong—the mantis is able to make big leaps, either to attack prey or to launch itself into flight.

Male mantids, like this one, have eight abdominal segments, whereas females have only six. Even so, the male is smaller than the female.

What's on the menu?

The mantis has a big appetite and typically feeds on flying insects, such as flies and moths. Larger mantis species may even attack and consume birds, small mammals, and lizards. As its prey draws near, the mantis sways from side to side before lashing out at lightning speed. The swaying helps pinpoint the precise position of the target, and the strike, when it comes, is deadly accurate. The mantis grasps the victim securely and bites into its neck, killing it quickly and efficiently.

STATISTICS

NAME:
Idolomantis diabolica

LIFE SPAN: 1.5 years

DISTRIBUTION: Southern & eastern Africa

STATUS: Unknown

SIZE: 3–4 in (8–10 cm)

Flying fox hanging Out

Photographing the Rodrigues flying fox was a privilege. The wild population of less than 1,000 individuals lives on just one tiny island. The bat's problems began with hunting and habitat loss. These reduced numbers to a level where natural events, like storms, threatened to finish them off. Zoos in Europe and North America now breed the species to try and save it from oblivion.

The bat's thumbs are free of the wing membrane. Each has a stout claw, used for climbing. The second finger of each wing also has a claw, used like a little knife to slit open fruits that would otherwise be too large for the bat to bite into.

Bats roost (rest) hanging from their feet. Special valves in the arteries and veins prevent too much blood from rushing to the head.

The long, pointed snout gives this group of bats the common name flying foxes. They are also known as fruit bats because most species eat fruit.

Noisy neighbors

Flying foxes live in colonies called roosts or camps. They hang upside down in tall trees and squabble noisily and almost nonstop. Crash-landings are a major cause of commotion—the bats are elegant in the air, but find landing tricky. Just as the colony settles after one incident, another seems to begin. It's a wonder any of them ever get any sleep.

Like most bats, flying foxes are nocturnal. They have good eyesight that makes the most of low-light conditions. Their sense of smell is also excellent.

STATISTICS

NAME:
Pteropus rodricensis
LIFE SPAN: 20 years

DISTRIBUTION: Rodrigues Island, Indian Ocean

STATUS: Critically endangered

SIZE: Wingspan 27 in (70 cm)

Flying fox food never tries to escape, so flying foxes' sense of hearing doesn't need to be acute and their ears are relatively small. Rodrigues flying foxes cannot use echolocation, the special bat sense used by insect-eating bats (see the Pipistrelle on page 64), but their excellent night vision and smell give them the sensory information they need.

The dark skin of the bat's wings is stretched between the long fingers of the hand and the ankles. At rest the wings are wrapped around the body, Dracula style.

Fruity feast

Flying foxes eat a variety of plant foods, including pollen, nectar, flower heads, and fruit. The bats' teeth and jaws are not well suited to chewing, so they pick only very soft, ripe fruits. Favorites are mangoes, bananas, and figs, which the bats mash to a pulp with their teeth and claws, and slurp up with their tongue. They spit out any hard pits or pieces of tough fruit skin.

The tip of each leg ends in strong claws. The phasmid uses these to attach itself firmly to its food plant, and often dangles upside down.

The phasmid adopts this threatening posture, with front legs and abdomen raised, whenever it is disturbed.

Antenna

These mobile palps are used for sampling and grasping food, which is clipped from the plant and pulped by the short powerful jaws beneath.

Color morphs
Giant prickly phasmids come in several color varieties, or morphs. This pale individual is very rare. Its cousins come in a range of leafy hues including brown, yellow, and tan. All provide wonderful camouflage.

Prickly phasmid

This thorny handful is a Giant prickly phasmid. Females grow to the size of a man's hand. Phasmids are often referred to as stick insects, though this species definitely looks more like a clump of leaves than a stick. Impressive camouflage is only one of the bizarre and wonderful adaptations exhibited by this extraordinary insect. It also has a kick like a mule, can reproduce without mating, and actively encourages ants to kidnap its young.

Foster par-ants
The female phasmid lays one egg a day, and flicks each one away so that it falls onto the ground below. Each egg resembles a small seed with a little stalklike growth called the capitulum. Before long, the eggs are found by ants, which carry them away to their nest. The ants eat the capitulum but the egg remains intact. Hidden away in the ant nest it develops safe from the attentions of predators and parasitic wasps. When the phasmid larva hatches, it looks like a small ant, but it soon leaves the nest to search for food. In its first molt it sheds its antlike appearance and becomes spiky and leafy.

Virgin births
Wild populations of Giant prickly phasmids contain many more females than males. Phasmid females who cannot find a male can produce eggs that will hatch. These take up to nine months to hatch (six months longer than fertilized eggs), and the young that emerge are always female.

In addition to offering physical protection, the spiny flanges (outgrowths) on the legs also add to the phasmid's camouflage, creating the impression of prickly leaves.

The phasmid's hind legs are extremely powerful. If approached too closely, the insect will kick violently enough to deter many insect eating animals, such as possums.

STATISTICS

DISTRIBUTION: Northeastern Australia & New Guinea

NAME:
Extatosoma tiaratum
LIFE SPAN: About 1 year

STATUS: Unknown

SIZE: 4–7 in (10–17 cm)

The wing buds of this almost mature female will never develop into proper wings. She cannot fly and will rely on her camouflage and spines to protect her during a life spent stepping carefully from food plant to food plant. Male Giant prickly phasmids have long wings and put them to good use taking short flights as they seek out a mate.

Shy seahorse

The scientific name for seahorses, *Hippocampus*, comes from the Greek words for "horse" (*hippus*) and "sea monster" (*campus*). It's hard to imagine anything less monstrous than this delicate and sedate little animal, but from the perspective of a tiny brine shrimp, the seahorse is a lurking menace. All but invisible among the weed, it is able to strike with astounding speed. What's more, the seahorse has relatively little to fear from predators. Its bony body contains hardly any muscle, and so it is not meaty enough to make a worthwhile meal.

Expectant father
It's not unusual among fish for males to care for the young, but seahorse fathers take their babysitting duties to such an extreme that it is they, not the females, that become pregnant. At spawning time, the female seahorse sheds her eggs into a special pouch on the male's belly, where his sperm fertilize them and they develop into larvae. Over the next three weeks his belly swells until the young are ready to be born.

This species of seahorse, sometimes called the Spiny seahorse, is decorated with many spines and frills, known as cirri, which help disguise its outline.

STATISTICS

NAME:
Hippocampus guttulatus
LIFE SPAN: 5 years

SIZE: 6–7 in (16–18 cm)

DISTRIBUTION: Eastern Atlantic & Mediterranean

STATUS: Unknown

The large eyes on the sides of the head can move independently, like those of the chameleon on page 78. When it spots prey such as a tiny shrimp, the seahorse can whip its snout around and attack with a suck-and-snap action. Amazingly, for a fish that does everything else at such a ponderous pace, the meal is gone in a few hundredths of a second. This is one of the fastest feeding of all vertebrate animals.

The seahorse uses its dorsal (back) fin to propel itself through the water. The small size of the fin, and the seahorse's unusual body shape, make it a very feeble swimmer—it can manage only about 6 ft (2 m) an hour.

A gas-filled buoyancy organ known as the swimbladder is located in the neck, helping the seahorse float upright in the water.

Male seahorses brood their developing young in a pouch on the belly.

The tail is unusual among fish in being prehensile, or able to grip. The seahorse coils its tail around seaweed or sea grass stems to anchor itself in one spot.

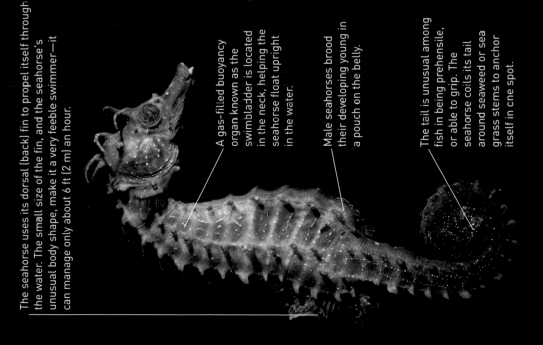

Hanging around

The seahorse's digestive system is simple but inefficient, and much of what is eaten passes straight through its body as waste. In order to get by, seahorses adopt a low-energy lifestyle, spending most of their time bobbing among fronds of algae. Using the tail as a tether saves energy that would be used swimming against the current, and the gas-filled swimbladder in the upper body helps the seahorse maintain its upright posture effortlessly.

Goliath bird eater

Bird-eating spiders, also referred to as tarantulas, are the world's largest spiders. They are also among the longest lived arthropods—in captivity a well-cared-for female can live 30 years. In the wild they live in dry forest or scrub, hiding by day in a burrow and emerging at dusk to lurk among the vegetation, waiting for dinner to pass by. This species is capable of tackling a variety of invertebrate prey, and sometimes also takes small birds, lizards, and mammals, striking them down with its front legs and inflicting a deadly bite with the poison-tipped fangs on its chelicerae, or mouthparts.

The spider adopted this classic threat posture when my camera lens came a bit too close for comfort. It's an aggressive-looking stance, with the front legs, pedipalps, and chelicerae all raised as though ready to strike. You'll see a cornered house spider do exactly the same thing.

Fragile existence
Tarantulas may be large, and very frightening to some people, but they are, in fact, extremely delicate animals. Their rigid body covering (exoskeleton) is thin and brittle, and may crack if the spider falls or is dropped. The exoskeleton is a fixed size and does not stretch, so the spider must shed it (molt) every now and then in order to grow.

Scarily hairy
Contrary to most people's expectation, the most offensive thing about a close encounter with a tarantula may not be a bite, but a nasty rash. In several New World species the back is covered in very tiny barbed hairs, a bit like those on the leaves of stinging plants. The hairs detach very easily and can embed themselves in skin or in the nose and throat, causing itching and allergic reactions in some people.

The spider's body is covered in fine hairs, which help the spider feel its surroundings. They are sensitive to touch and vibrations, and allow the spider to track passing prey accurately even though its eyesight is very poor.

The legspan of spiders is measured from the tip of one front leg to the tip of the back leg on the same side. This individual had a legspan of 8 in (20 cm), but might one day grow as large as 18 in (45 cm), bigger than a family-size pizza.

How many legs?
Everyone knows a spider has eight legs, but you could be forgiven for thinking you can see ten, or even twelve here. The leglike structures near the front are actually mouthparts—a pair of long, mobile pedipalps and a pair of short, fang-bearing chelicerae.

The undersides of the last two segments on each foot are covered with a patch of microscopic hairs called scopulae. These help the spider grip surfaces that feel perfectly smooth to our comparatively clumsy fingers.

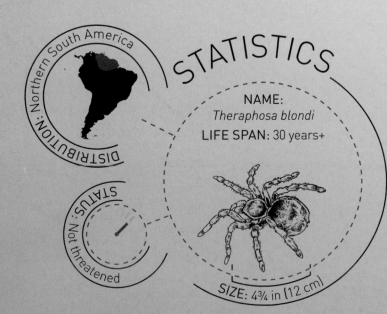

DISTRIBUTION: Northern South America

STATISTICS

NAME:
Theraphosa blondi
LIFE SPAN: 30 years+

STATUS: Not threatened

SIZE: 4¾ in (12 cm)

The velvety pedipalps are used as feelers and for gripping prey. The male tarantula also uses them to grip the female while mating. When moving around the forest, the spider habitually waves its pedipalps in front of its face, like a person feeling his way in the dark.

The spider's leg muscles only work one way—to bend the joints. When the spider wants to straighten its leg, it relies on hydraulic pressure, pumping blood into the leg until it unfolds—a bit like a balloon being inflated by air pressure.

Silky lining
Tarantulas spin silk from small structures called spinnerets located near the tip of the abdomen. But instead of weaving webs, they use the silk to line burrows where they rest. When hunting, they ambush prey by springing on it instead of snaring it with a web.

Spider bodies have two main parts (insects have three). The bulbous abdomen, or opisthosoma, is separated from the combined head and thorax, or prosoma, by a narrow waist.

The muscular chelicerae perform a variety of functions. The formidable fangs are used to subdue prey, piercing skin or exoskeletons and delivering a dose of toxin. Fortunately, the venom is not really dangerous to humans—bites are normally no more severe than a wasp or bee sting. When the prey is immobilized or dead, the spider uses its fangs to mash the body into a pulp for easy consumption.

The Goliath bird eater's legs are incredibly hairy. The hairs help the spider feel its way in the dark.

Red-eyed tree frog

This iconic amphibian lives in rain forests of Central and northern South America, and though not currently listed as endangered itself, it has become a symbol of the fight to conserve its threatened habitat. Red-eyed tree frogs are nocturnal and spend most of their time up in the trees, only venturing down to the ground at night to bathe in pools of water. They hunt by ambush, waiting patiently for passing prey. Victims are swiped from the vegetation or from midair with a long, sticky tongue and quickly engulfed in the frog's huge mouth.

Tree frogs eat mostly insects, such as this fly, but will consume anything that fits in their mouths, including smaller frogs.

Frogs typically have a wide mouth and a large gullet (throat) that allows them to swallow surprisingly large prey. Sometimes the frog will use its feet to help cram unwilling victims ins de. Frog teeth are tiny, and used only to grip prey. They are useless for chewing, so all meals are swallowed whole.

The frog's green color changes according to the temperature, its mood, and also at different times of the day.

At rest, the frog closes its eyes and retracts them into its skull. The mottled green eyelids help complete the frog's camouflage.

STATISTICS

NAME:
Agalychnis callidryas

LIFE SPAN: 5 years

SIZE: 2–3 in (5–7 cm)

DISTRIBUTION: Southern Mexico to northern South America

STATUS: Low risk

Red for danger
The green upper body provides excellent camouflage during the day, when the frog sleeps with its colorful legs tucked away and its eyes closed. If disturbed, however, the red eyes flick open. Together with a disorientating flash of colors from the legs as it jumps, this is often enough to startle a predator for the split second the frog needs to leap away. At night, a brief glimpse of the frog's bright colors can leave a confusing ghost image burned into the retinas of the predator's eyes, prompting a futile strike even after the target has gone.

The frog uses its skin to breathe. To absorb oxygen from the air efficiently, the skin must be moist, so the frog can survive only in the humid conditions of the rain forest.

Reproduction

During the rainy season, male frogs fight for the attention of females. The successful male will cling onto the female's back for many hours until she releases her eggs onto a leaf overhanging a puddle or pool. When the fertilized eggs rupture, the tadpoles are washed down the leaf into the water below, where they remain until they grow limbs and can climb up into the safety of the trees above.

Sticky pads on the end of each toe provide extraordinary grip on wet leaves and branches. Under a microscope the skin of the pads is seen to be made up of tall cells, which only attach at the base. The tip of each cell is free to fit closely with minute bumps in the climbing surface.

The feet are also important for grooming. The frog uses them to clean its body and wipe waxy secretions over its skin to condition it.

The frog's long limbs are perfectly adapted for climbing and jumping around trees.

Hawk moth

This magnificent creature, known as the Elephant hawk moth, is one of the world's fastest flying insects. It can speed through the air at up to 30 mph (50 kph), and fly for hours without rest. Like a hawk, it can hover midair, poised over flowers while it probes them for nectar, and can rapidly change direction to avoid predators, such as birds or bats.

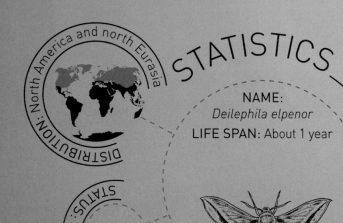

STATISTICS

DISTRIBUTION: North America and north Eurasia

NAME:
Deilephila elpenor
LIFE SPAN: About 1 year

STATUS: Not threatened

SIZE: Wingspan 2–2¾ in (5–7 cm)

The moth's long, flexible proboscis, or tongue, helps it to reach nectar at the bottom of deep flower tubes. It is coiled at rest, but when unfurled, the proboscis is at least as long as the rest of the body.

The moth's legs are long and strong. Each flight begins with a powerful thrust, which propels the moth into the air.

Hawk moths have significantly larger eyes than other moth species. They are also the only creatures we know of that are able to see full color at night.

Quick-change artist
The hawk moth caterpillar gives the adult moth its common name because it resembles the snout of an elephant's trunk. If threatened, the caterpillar reacts quickly. It rears up and pumps its head full of fluids so that it swells dramatically and displays startling eyelike markings. It looks very much like an angry snake and not surprisingly most birds and other would-be predators back off fast.

Moths use their antennae like a gyroscope in an airplane, to tell them which way up they are and in which direction they are facing. The antennae also pick up flower scents and chemical signals released by other moths.

Preflight checks

Before the moth can become airborne it has to warm up its flight muscles. It does this by contracting all its wing muscles simultaneously, so they pull against each other. This generates a lot of heat but not much movement. In flight, the muscles contract alternately, causing the wings to beat more than 50 times a second. The heat generated can boost the moth's body temperature to around 104°F (40°C).

The moth's vivid color may help to disguise it while it rests among the bright pink flowers of its main food plant, fireweed (rosebay willowherb).

The hairs that cover the moth's body and legs are, in fact, fine scales. They help the moth to keep warm at night and provide protection against predators, which end up with a mouthful of hair. They also help prevent the moth from becoming stuck in spider webs.

The tip of each tarsus (foot) is equipped with fine claws, with which the moth can anchor itself to any slightly rough surface.

Rhinoceros beetle

Rhinoceros beetles belong to the scarab family, and they are among the largest and heaviest insects on Earth. Zoologists have always been awed by this group of invertebrates, and closely related species have been given evocative names such as Goliath, Hercules, and Atlas. All these beetles are phenomenally powerful, able to lift several hundred times their own body weight. They can also be surprisingly noisy—adults produce a screeching sound by rubbing their wing cases against the armor plating of the thorax.

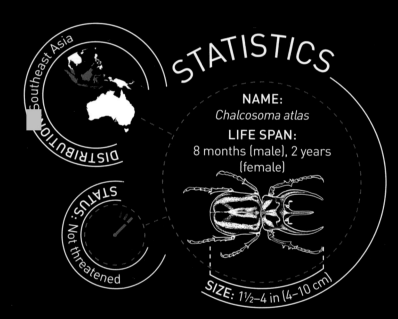

STATISTICS

DISTRIBUTION: Southeast Asia

STATUS: Not threatened

NAME:
Chalcosoma atlas

LIFE SPAN:
8 months (male), 2 years (female)

SIZE: 1½–4 in (4–10 cm)

The shape and size of the horns is related to the quality of the food supply as the beetle was growing up. It takes a lot of protein to build such magnificent armor, so only the best-fed grubs go on to develop such large horns. _____

Rotten nurseries
Like most scarabs, rhinoceros beetles begin life as a grub, hatching from an egg laid in either a ball of dung, or in rotting plant matter—dead wood is a favorite. They then spend a few months to several years eating and growing, in some cases as long as a human hand, before metamorphosing into an adult beetle. The adults, which live only a few months, fly short distances to find a mate. Males battle over dung piles or rotten logs. The winners mate with females, who excavate new nurseries where the next generation will start the cycle again.

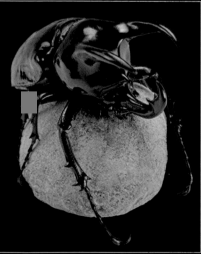

Atlas beetles create their dung balls from the droppings of large mammals, such as cattle. As they roll the dung to a safe place for laying eggs, it forms a neat ball.

The horns are rather blunt, with side branches, indicating they are used for wrestling rather than jousting or stabbing. Battles between male rhinoceros beetles are usually trials of strength rather than fights to the death.

The carapace gleams like a shiny new sports car. The microscopic structure of the cuticle reflects light, and the finishing touch is a thin layer of waxy water-proofing.

Rows of bristles protect all the beetle's joints, preventing them from becoming clogged with dirt.

The palps are covered in sensory hairs and pits, which can detect minute quantities of chemicals. They do the job of nostrils and taste buds.

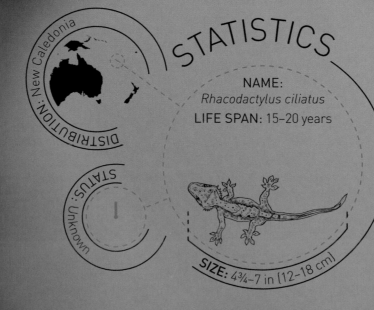

STATISTICS

DISTRIBUTION: New Caledonia

STATUS: Unknown

NAME:
Rhacodactylus ciliatus
LIFE SPAN: 15–20 years

SIZE: 4¾–7 in (12–18 cm)

Bright eyes
Unlike many other lizards, geckos have no eyelids and are unable to blink. In other animals, blinking keeps the eyes moist and cleans away particles of dirt. The gecko has a special transparent scale, called the spectacle, over each eye (though it is actually more like a contact lens), to keep moisture in and offer some protection. The job of cleaning the eyes is done by the long tongue!

The beautiful marbled eyes bulge out to the sides of the head, giving the gecko a very wide field of vision. In bright light, tiny muscles close the pupil to a narrow slit so that the gecko isn't dazzled.

Crested gecko

Twenty years ago, conservationists feared that this wonderful little reptile was extinct. But in 1994 it was rediscovered on the South Pacific islands of New Caledonia. It does well in captivity and is a popular pet with reptile keepers. The wild population still faces many challenges, especially from fire ants introduced to the islands—the ants compete with the geckos for food and can even kill them with their stinging bites.

These strange, eyelashlike growths are an extension of the crests that run along the body. They probably protect the gecko's eyes from damage as it pushes past leaves and tackles prey.

Crested geckos are a dull shade of yellow, gray, brown, or red. These are common colors among other gecko species, too, although some are bright green, and a few have the ability to change color to match their surroundings.

A moist tongue serves many useful purposes, from licking drops of water from leaves to flicking small insects into the mouth. It's also used for cleaning the face and body.

A light bite
Not all geckos have teeth, and those of the Crested gecko are very small. Most gecko jaws are too weak to be used for tearing up large prey. Instead, they target very small insects, and crush them slowly before swallowing them whole.

The jaws are lined with tiny teeth. They're not particularly sharp, but they do an important job, gripping prey until it stops struggling.

Spiked hedgehog

Unmistakeable among European mammals, the hedgehog is an ancient species, distantly related to shrews and moles. In addition to their quirky appearance, hedgehogs have many traits that endear them to people. They are easy to watch, they appreciate being fed (ideally with dry cat food, not milk), and they perform valuable pest control services in the garden, devouring snails and slugs with gusto.

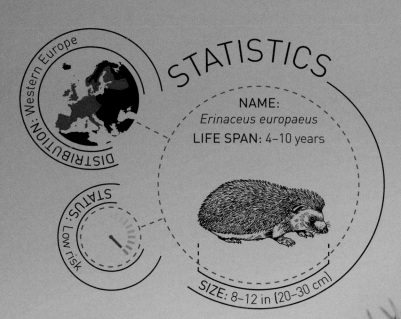

DISTRIBUTION: Western Europe

STATISTICS

NAME:
Erinaceus europaeus
LIFE SPAN: 4–10 years

STATUS: Low risk

SIZE: 8–12 in (20–30 cm)

Hibernation

In late fall, hedgehogs seek a secure but well ventilated spot, such as a dense hedge or bramble thicket, in which to hibernate. Hibernation is a state of extreme inactivity, which saves energy at times when food is too scarce to sustain life. A hibernating hedgehog drops its body temperature from 95°F (35°C) to match the surroundings, stopping just short of freezing point. The heart rate may fall as low as 12 beats per minute and breathing also slows dramatically. A hedgehog can lose one-third of its fall body weight during hibernation.

Hedgehogs often carry fleas, but these belong to a type that cannot survive on other animals like dogs, cats, or humans.

Hedgehogs have small eyes and limited color vision. The senses of hearing and smell, however, are very good.

Hedgehogs eat invertebrates such as beetles, slugs, and snails. They detect much of their food by smell. The moist black nose is constantly busy—in fact, hedgehogs are often heard before they are seen, giving away their position in the undergrowth with surprisingly noisy snuffling and snorting sounds.

Curling up

Hedgehogs possess a band of muscle around their body which, when tightened, pulls in a skirt of loose skin like a drawstring bag. At the same time, the spines are erected, turning the hedgehog into a prickly ball. Very few predators have mastered the art of opening rolled hedgehogs, but, sadly, the trick offers no protection against speeding cars.

Hidden from view under its spines, the hedgehog's legs are surprisingly long, allowing it to run at human walking pace. The feet have strong claws, used for digging.

Each spine is a greatly enlarged hair, made of keratin, the same protein found in all mammal fur.

The hedgehog can contract small muscles in its skin to make its spines stand on end. A similar system of muscles causes goosebumps in humans and the hackles to rise on an angry dog's neck. In all three species the reaction can be triggered by fear or anxiety.

Hog in a froth

People sometimes see hedgehogs apparently foaming at the mouth and worry that they are sick. In fact, this is a natural behavior, in which the hedgehog produces lots of frothy saliva, then spreads it avidly over its spines. This so-called self-annointing routine seems to be triggered when the animal encounters a new scent, but zoologists remain puzzled as to its actual purpose.

An adult hedgehog has between 5,000 and 7,000 spines. All are firmly embedded in the skin and do not drop out easily like the quills of a porcupine.

Camel spider

An encounter with this species would be a stern test for anyone with a fear of spiders. Its appearance is the stuff of nightmares and wild stories about its habits abound. But most of these are highly exaggerated. The camel spider is not venomous, and does not leap up to attack camels or people. It eats only termites or other small invertebrates. It's not even really a spider. In fact, it belongs to a related group of desert-dwelling arachnids more correctly known as solpugids.

The body is covered with stiff hairs, which the nocturnal camel spider uses like whiskers to help feel its way in the dark.

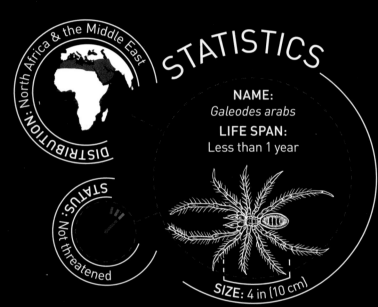

STATISTICS

DISTRIBUTION: North Africa & the Middle East

STATUS: Not threatened

NAME:
Galeodes arabs
LIFE SPAN:
Less than 1 year

SIZE: 4 in (10 cm)

Together with the muscles controlling them, the camel spider's mouthparts are among the largest in the animal kingdom, relative to its body size.

The pincerlike jaws, or chelicerae, are used for grappling with prey, then mashing it into a pulp before it is eaten. The camel spider may remove any very hard body parts before converting the rest into a sort of smoothie, which can be sucked up and digested easily. The chelicerae can also be rubbed together to produce soft calls a bit like those given by grasshopper.

Extra legs?
Solpugids look like 10-legged spiders, but only the hindmost three pairs of legs are used for running. The front pair are not true legs but pedipalps, which have sticky suckers at the tips, used for climbing smooth surfaces and for trapping prey. Behind them, the first pair of true legs serves as feelers, which the camel spider carries aloft as it scurries along.

A female
camel spider

Hermit crabs

Unlike true crabs, hermits have a body that is long and soft. Very wisely, they keep their vulnerable rear end tucked away inside a portable house made from an empty mollusk shell. As they grow, they are forced to move house, a dangerous and stressful business. Hermits are often found in enormous numbers—I encountered this pair scuttling around on a beach in Indonesia along with thousands of others.

The external shape or color of a shell does not matter too much to a hermit crab, but it's important that the inside of the shell coils to the right, the same way as the crab's body. Fortunately for the hermits, left-handed shells are very rare in nature—they would be extremely uncomfortable!

Only three of the hermit crab's five pairs of legs emerge from the shell. The first pair bear impressive pincers. Pairs two and three are long with slender points, ideal for scuttling on tiptoe over uneven surfaces.

The pincers, or chelae, look formidable but are rarely used in an attack. The left one is much larger than the right and is used for signaling, tearing up food, and for barricading the crab inside its shell when it feels threatened.

Mobile home

Most hermit crabs use empty sea snail shells to protect their soft abdomen from predators, but other options include clam shells and hollow bamboo stalks—even plastic bottle tops will be tried on for size. Fights often break out over the most desirable shells. A hermit will try to carry the biggest house it can manage, in an effort to appear bigger and stronger than it really is. In a squabble over food or a mate, a small crab can sometimes bluff its way to success simply by having a bigger house than its rivals.

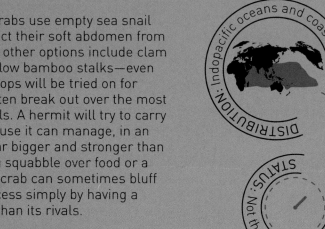

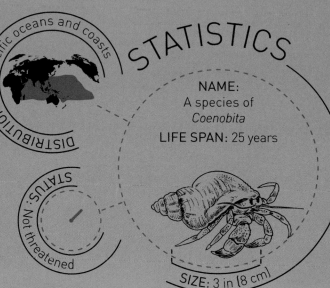

STATISTICS

DISTRIBUTION: Indopacific oceans and coasts

STATUS: Not threatened

NAME:
A species of
Coenobita
LIFE SPAN: 25 years

SIZE: 3 in (8 cm)

Diverse hermits

There are several hundred different species of hermit crab, many of which live permanently in the sea. The hermits in the picture, however, belong to a group known as land hermits, which have evolved the crustacean equivalent of lungs—enclosed gills that operate out of water as long as they have a humid environment to keep them moist and healthy.

Hermit crabs have sharp eyesight, and good night vision. Being nocturnal helps them avoid the heat of the sun, which can kill by drying out their delicate gills.

The fourth and fifth pairs of legs are much smaller than the front legs, and usually stay tucked away inside the shell. They help the crab grip its house and pick up and remove particles of dirt and debris from inside.

Hermit crabs have six separate pairs of mouthparts, each of which performs a different function—from grasping, feeling, and tasting to snipping, crushing, and stuffing. It's a bit like having 12 specialized pieces of cutlery to process every mouthful.

Hermit crabs have two pairs of antennae—one short, one long. These finely tuned sensors help the crab feel its way, test food, and pick up vibrations in both air and water.

Young grass snake

Grass snakes are common throughout Europe, except Ireland and northern Scandinavia. Females can grow well over 3 ft (1 m) long, but are rarely seen, since they are extremely shy. They are harmless to people, and easily distinguished from the venomous adder by their large size and distinctive yellow collar. Round pupils give the face a less sinister expression than that of the adder, which has the vertical slit pupils typical of vipers. This individual is only a few days old, and measured about 6½ in (16 cm) long when it hatched from the egg.

Water lover

The Grass snake could just as easily be known as the water snake, since it is nearly always found close to ponds or streams. Water is especially important for youngsters like this, since being small they are prone to dehydration (drying out). Grass snakes specialize in hunting amphibians such as frogs and newts. A tadpole makes a worthwhile snack, but a full-grown adult frog will keep a Grass snake going for months. Snakes swallow their prey whole.

The scales of a Grass snake are smooth and shiny. They feel cool and polished, and not at all slimy.

DISTRIBUTION: Europe except Ireland & N Scandinavia

STATISTICS

NAME:
Natrix natrix
LIFE SPAN: 15 years

STATUS: Low risk

SIZE: 27–47 in (70–120 cm)

The scales of young Grass snakes like this one are often tinged with blue, which fades as they grow older and shed their skin.

The bright eyes see well at close range, and are especially good at detecting movement. They are covered with transparent scales, known as spectacles. These become milky when the snake is ready to molt and are shed along with the rest of the skin.

Dead ringer

Grass snakes are great actors. If cornered, their first reaction is to rear up and pretend to strike, like a venomous viper. If this fails to deter an attacker, the snake will suddenly convulse as if in agony, then flop sideways, mouth gaping and tongue lolling. It looks stone dead and does not flinch when touched. As a finishing touch, the snake releases a stomach-churning stench from glands near the start of the tail. This is enough to make most predators lose their appetite and move on in search of a less revolting meal. Then the snake comes miraculously back to life and slithers on its way, none the worse for wear.

The snake has a blue-black forked tongue, which flickers constantly, in and out of its mouth. The tongue collects scents from air and water and transfers them to a scent detector in the mouth called the vomeronasal organ.

The snake breathes through its nostrils, but they are less important for smelling than the tongue.

The whole body is sensitive to vibrations in the ground, which the snake uses to sense the approach of predators or prey.

Young snakes like this one molt (shed their skin) every few months. The interval between molts increases with age. Adult male Grass snakes molt twice a year, females only once.

Pipistrelle

STATISTIC

NAME:
Pipistrellus pipistrellus

LIFE SPAN: 5–15 years

SIZE: Wingspan 7–9 in (18–24 cm)

DISTRIBUTION: Europe except N Scandinavia

STATUS: Low Risk

I encountered this feisty fellow clinging to a crevice in tree bark. I took the shot quickly, because he was obviously annoyed by the disturbance— he hissed continually until I went away. A few years ago this species could be easily identified simply as a pipistrelle, but in 1997 zoologists realized that what they had thought was a single species of bat was, in fact, two. They look virtually identical and can usually be separated only by their calls, which are given at different frequencies. The high-pitched caller is known as the Soprano pipistrelle, and its deeper voiced cousin is the Common pipistrelle.

Home to roost

Female pipistrelles usually roost, or rest, in large groups, often in large tree holes or roof spaces. In summer these roosts become busy nurseries in which the females give birth and rear their young. Males tend to live alone or in much smaller groups, but in winter both sexes gather in mixed colonies which can include anything up to 100,000 bats.

Despite its dense, fluffy fur, the bat's mouselike body loses heat energy fast. Combined with the enormous energy cost of flying, this means pipistrelles have huge appetites. A single individual will catch and eat up to 3,000 insects in a single night's hunting.

How small?

Bats are among the smallest, lightest mammals on Earth. An adult pipistrelle weighs about 0.2 oz (6 g) and can squeeze through gaps barely more than ½ in (15 mm) across. But it's a heavyweight compared to the Bumblebee bat from Thailand. Weighing only 0.07 oz (2 g), this minute creature is also the world's smallest mammal.

The huge ears are sensitive enough to pick up the minute echoes of insects such as mosquitoes, midges, and moths.

Seeing with sound

Bats are not blind, but in complete darkness these nocturnal animals have to rely completely on sound to find their way. In a process known as echolocation, the bat gives special high-pitched calls, which reflect, or bounce, off objects nearby, producing echoes. The bat's huge ears receive these reflected sound waves and the brain uses them to build a sound picture of the surroundings, including its prey. It's an extraordinary skill.

Needle-sharp teeth allow the bat to snap up flying insects, killing them instantly. Most meals are eaten while the bat is in flight, and inedible parts, such as wings, are dropped.

Bat wings are supported by the same set of bones your have in your hand. Four fingers form a spindly scaffold, like the struts of an umbrella. The bones are linked by a web of fine skin called the wing membrane, or pataguim.

Deafening squeaks

Small bats like pipistrelles belong to a group zoologists call the Vespertilionidae, from the Latin *vesper,* meaning "evening," which is when they emerge. We can't hear the echolocation calls of evening bats, but they are anything but quiet. The shout of the pipistrelle is about 120 decibels, as loud as a fire alarm held next to your ear! But we're not deafened when a pipistrelle zooms overhead, because its cries are so high-pitched they are ultrasonic and fall well outside our hearing range. Children have sharper ears than adults and can sometimes detect bat calls as a faint clicking.

A stickleback for supper

This scene of carnage is a reminder that the struggle to survive is universal in the living world. The tension and drama of life in the pond near my office is every bit as epic as that on the African plains, in the jungles of Asia and South America, or in shark-infested seas around the world. These two are worthy adversaries. The fish is sleek and fast, with armor plating and needlelike spines to protect it. On another day it might have escaped the stick bug, or eaten its eggs or young. But today the invertebrate is the victor, using stealth and precision to find a fatal chink in the stickleback's defenses.

The lateral line is a sense organ that runs along the flanks of fish. Cells called neuromasts in the lateral line detect vibrations and water movement, helping the fish recognize currents and sense the movement of other animals.

This species is known as the Three-spined stickleback. The spines offer protection against some large predators, which find the fish a painful mouthful, but they are easily avoided by the water stick bug.

Doting fathers
Male sticklebacks go to great lengths to attract a mate. They build a nest, perform an energetic courtship dance, drive off rivals, and then take on all the parenting duties. They guard their eggs gallantly, fan them continuously with oxygen-rich water, and keep them clean.

Large eyes serve the fish well in slightly gloomy water, but the stick bug's camouflage allowed it to sneak up unnoticed.

The bug pierces its victim with mouthparts that are fused to form a needlelike weapon known as a stylet. The stylet doubles as a drinking straw through which body fluids are sucked.

The stickleback's flanks are armored with bony plates. Freshwater varieties have fewer than 10 plates, but the sticklebacks that go to sea may have as many as 40.

Seeing red

In the mating season, male sticklebacks develop a bright red belly and chin. The color helps attract females, but other males also react to it. In fact, males in breeding condition become very agitated at the sight of anything red, because they associate it with potential rivals. The famous Dutch zoologist Niko Tinbergen discovered this when the sticklebacks he kept in a tank on his windowsill went crazy every day when a red mail truck drove by!

The stick bug flies well. Its wings are kept folded neatly along its body while it remains under water, but it will emerge at night to fly in search of other pools with good hunting or mating opportunities.

Gangly legs help the stick bug clamber around on pond weed and other floating debris, but it is a poor swimmer.

Bottom up

The stick bug has no gills and cannot extract oxygen directly from the water. Instead it uses a snorkel-like breathing tube, the siphon, at the tip of its abdomen to breathe air from the surface.

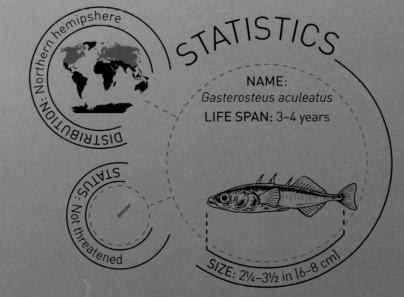

DISTRIBUTION: Northern hemipshere

STATISTICS

NAME:
Gasterosteus aculeatus
LIFE SPAN: 3–4 years

STATUS: Not threatened

SIZE: 2¼–3½ in (6–8 cm)

Gecko grip

Geckos are able to scurry up vertical surfaces as smooth as glass, and walk on ceilings as easily as they cross a floor—all without the aid of suckers or glue. Their agility can seem supernatural. They are welcome in houses because they feed on insect pests, including several that carry disease. A gecko indoors is said to bring luck, and the sound of a gecko's call is regarded as a good omen. Outside houses, geckos are often seen sunning themselves on rocks or logs. They rest in crevices or among dense vegetation.

In many gecko species the tail is tapered and as long as the rest of the body. Other geckos, sometimes known as knob-tails, have a very short, blunt tail.

In times of plenty, a gecko stores fat in its tail. This reserve of energy will help see it through lean times when food is scarce.

Most gecko species are able to regrow a new tail if the original one has been lost, a process that takes several weeks. The new tail is usually a different color from the rest of the body and contains cartilage instead of bone.

The gecko's toes are long, and they splay widely so that at least one or two on each foot can find firm footing even on very uneven surfaces.

The bones at the base of the tail have specially weakened spots, which the gecko can snap at will if it is grabbed by a predator. The severed tail may continue to twitch, distracting the predator long enough for the gecko to escape. Blood vessels in the tail stump close up so the gecko doesn't bleed to death.

The unusual toes of this fan-fingered gecko spread into two ridged pads. The extra surface area provided gives the gecko even better grip on smooth rock walls.

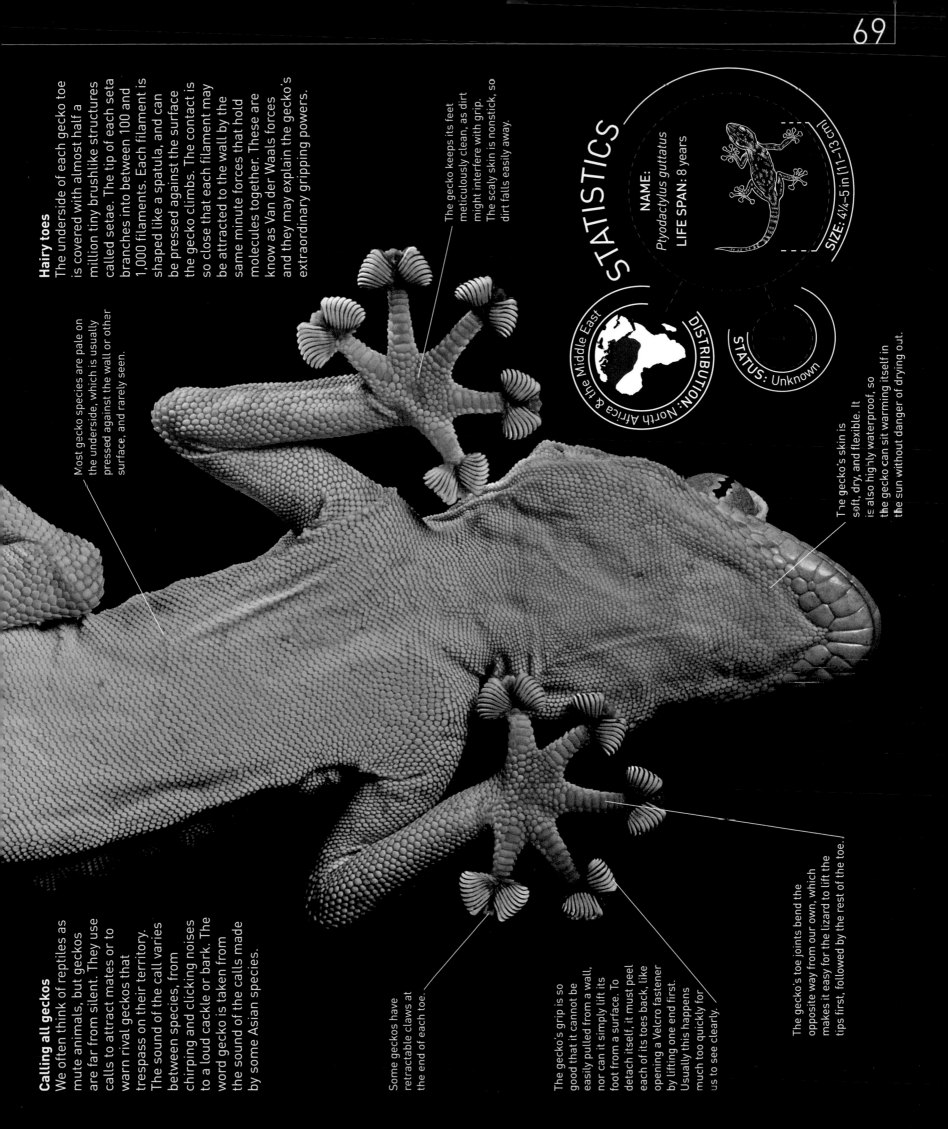

Hairy toes

The underside of each gecko toe is covered with almost half a million tiny brushlike structures called setae. The tip of each seta branches into between 100 and 1,000 filaments. Each filament is shaped like a spatula, and can be pressed against the surface the gecko climbs. The contact is so close that each filament may be attracted to the wall by the same minute forces that hold molecules together. These are know as Van der Waals forces and they may explain the gecko's extraordinary gripping powers.

Calling all geckos

We often think of reptiles as mute animals, but geckos are far from silent. They use calls to attract mates or to warn rival geckos that trespass on their territory. The sound of the call varies between species, from chirping and clicking noises to a loud cackle or bark. The word gecko is taken from the sound of the calls made by some Asian species.

Most gecko species are pale on the underside, which is usually pressed against the wall or other surface, and rarely seen.

The gecko keeps its feet meticulously clean, as dirt might interfere with grip. The scaly skin is nonstick, so dirt falls easily away.

The gecko's skin is soft, dry, and flexible. It is also highly waterproof, so the gecko can sit warming itself in the sun without danger of drying out.

Some geckos have retractable claws at the end of each toe.

The gecko's grip is so good that it cannot be easily pulled from a wall, nor can it simply lift its foot from a surface. To detach itself, it must peel each of its toes back, like opening a Velcro fastener by lifting one end first. Usually this happens much too quickly for us to see clearly.

The gecko's toe joints bend the opposite way from our own, which makes it easy for the lizard to lift the tips first, followed by the rest of the toe.

STATISTICS

NAME:
Ptyodactylus guttatus
LIFE SPAN: 8 years

DISTRIBUTION: North Africa & the Middle East

STATUS: Unknown

SIZE: 4¼–5 in (11–13 cm)

Colorful Gouldian finch

With his riotous plumage, whose rainbow hues include colors the human eye cannot even see, this male Gouldian finch really stands out from the crowd. Males of this species occur in three genetic color types, or morphs. The commonest type has a black head, the rarest has a yellow head. But it's the redheads that are the most dazzling, and they seem to know it, frequently pulling rank on less colorful rivals. Only very fit, healthy males can maintain such bright head plumage.

STATISTICS

NAME:
Erythrura gouldiae
LIFE SPAN: About 6 years

SIZE: 4¼–5 in [11–13 cm]

DISTRIBUTION: Northern Australia

STATUS: Endangered

This finch is a hothead in more ways than one. The temperament of male birds is related to head color. Only the most aggressive individuals produce this intense red and redheads dominate over males with a black or yellow head and those with a paler red head.

The stout beak is adapted for a specialty diet. The tip and edges work as both vice and chisel to split and prize open tough seed cases.

To other finches, this blue collar glows ultraviolet, a color humans cannot see because our eyes don't have the appropriate receptors.

The green sheen of the back feathers is created by a combination of blue light scattered by the fine structure of the feathers and an overlying yellow pigment.

Dwindling numbers

The Gouldian finch is popular with breeders, and tens of thousands live in captivity around the world. But these numbers hide a sad reality—the species is heading for extinction in the wild, with fewer than 10,000 adults remaining. The decline is linked to the increase in livestock farming in Australia—cattle and sheep remove early-seeding grasses on which the finches rely for food in the spring.

Finches belong to the huge order of birds known as passerines, or perching birds. Passerine feet are able to grip small branches, and the grappling-hook claws allow them to cling to vertical trunks with ease.

Stag beetle battles

Evolution sometimes does extraordinary things to animal bodies, but these beetles are among the strangest. The males, seen here, have grotesquely enlarged mouthparts. These have developed by a process zoologists call sexual selection—the characteristic is enhanced because it gives animals a better chance of winning a mate. There are about 1,200 stag beetle species living all over the world—this pair are from Indonesia.

The beetle's exoskeleton is made of very tough chitin. Adults do not molt (shed their exoskeleton) so once metamorphosis is complete they cannot grow any bigger.

The antennae have distinctive flattened tips, and are often bent or broken in tussles between males.

The antlers of the male stag beetle are overgrown mandibles, or jaws.

The branching prongs, known as tines, help rival males lock antlers as they attempt to wrestle each other from the log. Male deer (stags) have branching antlers for the same reason.

The beetle's head is full of muscles that operate the jaws. Despite their size, most male stag beetles cannot bite very hard. Females, however, need powerful cutting mouthparts for excavating nursery chambers in rotting wood. Although they have much smaller jaws, they can deliver a bite fierce enough to draw blood from human skin.

Showing off to the girls
Stag beetle battles are principally about defending territory, but the combatants are also motivated by a certain amount of macho bravado. In stag beetle mating systems, it's the females that make the final decision on who will father their offspring. So each male is eager to demonstrate his health and vigor in the hope that it will impress the ladies.

This beetle is about to be thrown to the ground in a humiliating defeat. He is unlikely to be seriously injured, but he might be more careful who he challenges in future.

Long-lived grubs
Like many insects, stag beetles spend much more of their lives as hungry grubs than as grown-up beetles. Adult females lay eggs in rotten wood, where the developing larvae may feed for several years.

The claws at the tip of each spindly leg look delicate, but they are very strong. This beetle is able to support his own weight and that of his rival with just four feet gripping the bark like grappling hooks.

How the battle began

STATISTICS
DISTRIBUTION: Indonesia

STATUS: Unknown

NAME:
Cyclommatus imperator
LIFE SPAN: 2.5–3.5 years

SIZE: 2½–3½ in (7–9 cm)

The delicate hindwings are folded neatly and tucked away under the front wings, which form tough covers known as elytra.

Moon jellyfish

This simple creature belongs to the Cnidaria—the same group as anemones and corals. The semitranslucent body allows a fascinating glimpse into the workings of an animal with no head, no brain, no circulation, no skeleton, and no skin. But don't be fooled by the simplicity—this basic body plan has worked perfectly for half a billion years, making jellyfish some of the most successful animals on Earth. What's more, they are highly effective predators, able to make a meal of many more complex life forms.

Dangerous beauty

The word Cnidaria comes from the Greek *cnid*, meaning "nettle." Jellyfish use venom to stun or kill their prey, and in self defense. The sting is delivered by special cells called cnidocytes. These can be anywhere on the body but tend to be concentrated in the tentacles. When triggered by touch, the cnidocyte throws out a tiny, venomous thread. The sting of the moon jellyfish is very mild and most people will scarcely feel it, but smaller animals including tiny fish, shrimps, and drifting larvae will be killed or paralyzed almost instantly.

The rim of the bell is fringed with very short, fine stinging tentacles.

Jellyfish have a funnel-like mouth, known as the manubrium, which opens in the middle of the underside. The mouth leads to a cavity inside the body called the coelenteron, which has four simple stomachs called gastric pouches.

The pink horseshoe-shaped structures are reproductive organs. These release eggs and sperm into the water through the jellyfish's mouth.

A network of canals radiates out from the gastric pouches, carrying essential nutrients to every part of the body.

Jellyfish have no gills or lungs. The whole body acts as a respiratory surface, meaning oxygen dissolved in seawater passes directly into the body. It reaches all the cells without the need for blood or a circulatory system to pump it.

Split personality

The two phases of the jellyfish life cycle are so distinct that they look like completely different organisms. The individual you see here is in the phase known as the medusa. Medusae are free-swimming and reproduce usually by releasing eggs and sperm. A fertilized egg develops into a larva called the planula, which settles on the seafloor and grows into a flower-shaped animal known as a polyp. In spring, the polyp begins budding off a series of tiny, saucerlike medusae, known as ephyra. The ephyra drift in the plankton and if they manage to avoid being eaten (often by other jellyfish) they will reach maturity after three or four months.

The bell is filled with a translucent jelly known as mesoglea or ectoplasma. It supports the body and gives the jellyfish its shape, but cannot do so out of water. A jellyfish washed up on a beach is a hopeless heap of mucus—a sorry sight indeed.

STATISTICS

NAME:
Aurelia aurita

LIFE SPAN: Up to 1 year

SIZE: Up to 12 in (30 cm)

DISTRIBUTION: Tropical & temperate oceans & seas

STATUS: Not threatened

Muscles in the rim of the bell contract, causing the body to pulse. On each contraction, water is pushed out of the bell, propelling the jellyfish upward. To move downward, the jellyfish stops pulsing and allows gravity to do the work.

Four long appendages, the oral arms, trail from the center of the bell. They are often mistaken for tentacles, but in fact, they are the jellyfish equivalent of lips. They help guide food into the manubrium, or mouth.

There are eight small nodes, known as rhopalia, spaced evenly around the edge of the bell-shaped body. These are jellyfish sense organs. Each rhopalium contains cells that detect chemicals, touch, gravity, and light. With this basic information the jellyfish can react to its environment—for example, by rising to the surface to feed at night, then sinking deeper by day, and by homing in on food.

Mantis mealtime

When I see one of these magnificent insects poised motionless with its great forelegs raised in front of its face, it's easy to imagine it is saying a prayer. In fact, this aggressive predator is more interested in preying than praying. As soon as a smaller creature comes within range, the mantis strikes. Its legs whip out to grab the victim and drag it head-first to its mouth—the motion is so fast that the human eye sees it only as a blur.

The powerful front legs are equipped with several sets of sharp spikes and thorns that grip prey firmly. There's no escape for this poor fly.

The mantis has no venom to subdue its prey, so it tackles the head-first, and the victim soon stops struggling. With its powerful mandibles (jaws) the mantis makes short work of its kill.

Masters of disguise
Most mantises use camouflage to blend in with their surroundings. You could be within inches of a mantis and never see it. Some species change color to blend in with their background and others have a body that mimics different flowers, blades of grass, twigs, leaves, or even other creatures such as ants.

Mantises smell by flicking their antennae to capture airborne scent molecules on fine sensory hairs.

Unlike most insects, a mantis can swivel its head all the way around, so it can look over its shoulder. Mantis eyes are very sensitive to movement and can spot predators or prey approaching from almost any direction.

Like predatory mammals and birds, mantises see in stereo, which means they are able to judge distances accurately. The compound eye is constructed of hundreds of narrow tubes called ommatidia. Each tube has a double, light-guiding lens on the outer end and light-sensitive cells at the base.

The swirls and stripes on mantis eyes add to the overall camouflage. The black dot in the center of the eye looks like a pupil, but in fact it's a glimpse of the dark bases of some of the tubes that make up the compound eye.

A dangerous game
Female praying mantises are famous for their habit of occasionally eating the males with which they mate. This seems to be particularly common in captive mantises, and in hungry ones. The female needs nutrients to produce healthy eggs, and the male must approach carefully if he is to escape becoming her next meal. Some male mantises seem able to avoid being attacked by distracting the female with a long drawn-out courtship dance.

A mantis hears through a slit between its front legs. It can detect ultrasonic frequencies, including the calls of hunting bats, which prey on mantises.

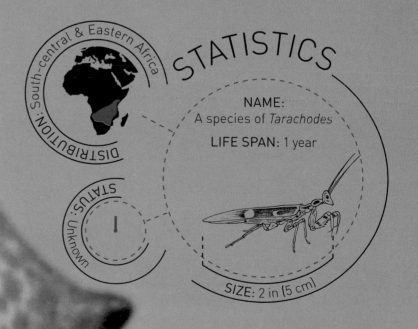

STATISTICS

DISTRIBUTION: South-central & Eastern Africa

STATUS: Unknown

NAME: A species of *Tarachodes*

LIFE SPAN: 1 year

SIZE: 2 in (5 cm)

Moody Veiled chameleon

With their spooky swiveling eyes, their blink-and-you-miss-it hunting technique, and dramatic color changes, it's not surprising chameleons are often regarded as magical creatures. The colors sometimes help with camouflage, but their main function is communicating emotion. The pale green adopted by this female suggests she is fairly calm, but minutes later when I tried to pick her up, she went black with rage. As a pet, she's used to being handled occasionally, so I must have caught her on a bad day.

DISTRIBUTION: Yemen & southwestern Saudi Arabia

STATISTICS

NAME:
Chamaeleo calyptratus
LIFE SPAN: 5–8 years

STATUS
Not threatened

SIZE: 10–18 in (25–45 cm)

The highly mobile eyes are protected by thick lids, with a small opening for the pupil. Each eye can rotate independently in its socket, together giving an all-around 360° field of view. When prey is spotted, both eyes roll to the front to provide accurate judgment of range.

The tongue is an extraordinary weapon, able to shoot out and strike at prey up to three chameleon body-lengths away. The movement is controlled by a mechanism of muscle and bone in the throat called the hyoid apparatus, which uses tension to catapult the tongue with deadly accuracy. The tip of the tongue is supersticky.

Treetop stalker
Chameleons live in trees. The five toes on each foot are fused into twos and threes, creating a very strong pincer grip. The long, tapering tail is also prehensile and grasps branches for added security. Chameleons climb slowly, and pause often, especially when hunting. By swaying gently from side to side, the chameleon mimics the movement of a leaf in the breeze. Using this disguise it will stalk prey such as insects as they rest, striking when they are in range of the sticky tongue.

The so-called gular crest runs from the chin to the belly. It helps make the chameleon look bigger than it really is. If spotted by a predator, or confronting a rival, the chameleon will often turn sideways to maximize the appearance of bulk.

The bony crest, known as a casque, is unusually large in this species. Scientists think it may be used as an amplifier for buzzing communication calls. The casque of males tends to be taller than that of females like this one.

The outermost layer of skin is transparent. The chameleon's variable colors are created by pigment cells called chromatophores deeper in the skin. These expand and contract to display different intensities of color.

Dune tiger beetle

Meet the fastest predator on six legs. This powerful insect lives up to its name, using stealth and speed to deadly effect. Tiger beetles occur all over the world, favoring warm sandy habitats such as heathlands and dunes. There are between 1,400 and 2,000 different species, varying in size from ¼–2¼ in (6–60 mm). This handsome specimen, which I found in southern France, was a tricky model, dashing off at top speed or taking to the air whenever I tried to sneak close.

A glittering jewel

The beetle's exoskeleton is a lightweight suit of armor. It's a perfect fit and provides both support and protection. The green and gold color helps to camouflage the tiger among the sand dunes, while the gorgeous iridescent gleam reflects some of the sun's heat. The species' common name owes as much to the bold stripes across the wing cases as its fierce and athletic hunting behavior.

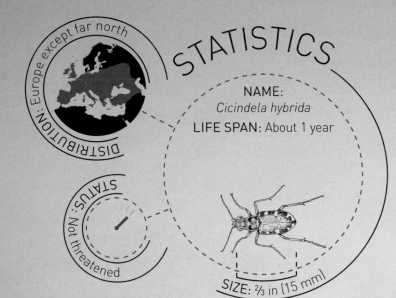

STATISTICS

DISTRIBUTION: Europe except far north

NAME:
Cicindela hybrida

LIFE SPAN: About 1 year

STATUS: Not threatened

SIZE: ⅔ in (15 mm)

Like all beetles, the tiger has two pairs of wings. The outer pair are hardened into armorlike wing cases called elytra. The second pair are much more delicate and are kept folded away when not in use.

The beetle's foot, or tarsus, is made up of five slim sections, but only the claws at the very tip touch the ground—this arrangement is similar to that seen in horses and antelope, which walk on the tips of one or two toes per foot.

The next generation

Tiger beetles usually live alone and only seek out a mate when they are ready to breed. Males and females serenade each other by rubbing the top of their back legs against the edge of the wing case to make sweet beetle music! Once they have mated, the female digs a burrow where she will lay her eggs. Once hatched, the larvae are predators, too. They lurk at the burrow entrance waiting to grab any prey that wanders too close.

The beetle's underside is protected by a series of overlapping plates. These flex to allow movement when running or flying.

The beetle's head is encased in a close-fitting helmet made of six separate plates of exoskeleton.

These huge compound eyes allow the beetle to see forward, upward, and out to each side. This is the perfect setup for a hunter that also needs to keep a wary eye out for larger predators that might try to attack it from above.

Surprise attack
The tiger beetle lives in a tiny burrow dug into the sand. It lies in wait there until an unsuspecting victim walks by, then springs from the burrow to give chase at up to 8 ft (2.5 m) per second.

The tiger beetle uses its antennae to feel its way underground. The fine sensory hairs may also pick up scents carried in the air.

The mouthparts are immensely powerful, especially the mandibles, or jaws, which work with a pincer action. It's vital that the beetle makes its kills quickly and effectively, as a struggling victim might easily damage one of the long, delicate legs. A lame tiger beetle cannot hunt and is doomed.

Born to run
A quick look at a tiger beetle's legs makes it clear that it's built for speed. Compare these legs with those of a cheetah or a racehorse. They are all long (to maximize the distance covered with each stride) and slim, (to reduce weight and wind resistance). Look how the beetle stands on the tips of its claws, just as a human sprinter runs on his or her toes instead of flat feet.

Sensitive palps below the jaws feel and taste the prey and help the beetle decide what is edible. They are also used to hold and manipulate the captured prey.

Spines at the bottom of the beetle's tibia (the long fourth segment of the leg) make the beetle an uncomfortable mouthful for some would-be predators, and might act as a deterrent.

Tiger beetles can run on hot sand at temperatures of up to 127°F (53°C)—the hotter the sand, the faster they run!

The last segment of each leg, the pretarsus, has two claws which dig into the sand to provide grip.

Walking leaf insect

A moth-eaten old leaf, going brown around the edges, caught on a bramble as it fell from the tree... or is it? In fact, this is no leaf, but a leaf-eating insect. The Giant leaf phasmid is the largest of its kind and like other stick and leaf insects it completes its amazing disguise by swaying gently from side to side, like a leaf moving in the breeze. The species is virtually impossible to spot in the wild, but this nymph grew up in my studio so she was a bit easier to track down.

The art of invisibility
The word phasmid comes from the Latin *phasma*, meaning phantom. The leaf insect has mastered its disguise so perfectly that in its natural habitat it is effectively invisible. Zoologists call this disappearing act crypsis. Just like a cryptic crossword clue, the phasmid is hidden, and difficult to make out.

KEY STATISTICS

NAME:
Phyllium giganteum
LIFE SPAN: 14–15 months

SIZE: 4¾ in (12 cm)

DISTRIBUTION: Malaysia

STATUS: Unknown

At rest the leaf insect holds its front legs above its head, where they give the impression of a torn and withered leaf stem.

Nearly all leaf insects are female and they can reproduce without mating. Females always have short antennae like these. The very rare male leaf insects have long, hairy antennae, which they use for tracking down females.

Leaves rarely stay perfect for long, and the leaf insect convincingly mimics imperfections such as nibbled or torn margins and edges turning brown with age.

Safe and sound?
Exquisite camouflage keeps the phasmid safe from a great many predators that hunt by day, using sharp eyesight to detect prey. But at night a new threat emerges— bats hunt not by sight, but by sound, and can home in on a leaf insect using the tiny noises made by its jaws munching foliage.

The enormous flat flanges (outgrowths) on either side of the abdomen serve no other purpose than crypsis, but growing them uses a lot of body resources. The investment that the insect puts into perfecting its disguise shows the importance of camouflage to survival.

All the vital organs are crammed into the central part of the body. Here the central part of the abdomen is just visible, disguised as the leaf's midrib.

Blowfly birthday

A pupa is a miracle of packaging—it's hard to imagine that a fully formed adult insect is folded up inside, until you see it with your own eyes. The sight of a brand new adult struggling from its pupa is a piece of magic I never tire of witnessing. Blowflies are found everywhere, especially in summer. Adults live up to a month, during which time a female can lay up to 9,000 eggs. Maggots hatch and feed on rotting meat for a couple of days before finding somewhere dry to pupate. I kept this pupa for a couple of weeks, then grabbed my camera when I saw signs of life inside...

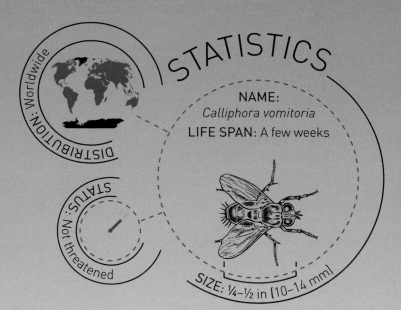

STATISTICS

DISTRIBUTION: Worldwide

STATUS: Not threatened

NAME:
Calliphora vomitoria
LIFE SPAN: A few weeks

SIZE: ¼–½ in (10–14 mm)

The hardened and now empty case in which the maggot turned into an adult fly is, in fact, the old skin. Looking carefully, you can see the rings marking the larval body segments.

From larva to fly
During pupation, the whole body of the maggot—except for crucial clusters of cells called imaginal disks—was completely liquefied within the pupal case, and the body of the adult fly was then reconstructed from this soup. The process of metamorphosis takes a couple of weeks to complete, although it depends on temperature. If it is too cold the adult will wait inside the pupal case until the weather warms.

Breaking out
In order to escape from the tight confines of the case in which it pupated, the young fly uses a special organ on its head called the ptilium. This pulsates, like a balloon being alternately inflated and deflated. Each pulse helps draw the body a little farther into the open. As soon as the legs are free, the fly can crawl out easily.

Getting up and ready
The complete process of emerging from a pupa is called eclosion. During the first 10 minutes after eclosion, body fluids are pumped into the veins of the crumpled wings, which stretch and straighten. Within another 10 minutes the wings harden and the insect is able to fly.

Completing the cycle
This brand new fly will be able to breed in just 24 hours. After mating, a female will seek out a suitable nursery in a nice piece of rotten meat or dung and lay her eggs in batches of about 300. The newly hatched maggots will immediately begin munching on the convenient food supply.

Tucked behind each wing is a small, drumstick-shaped structure called a haltere. Halteres act as stabilizers, flicking this way and that to keep the fly in balance as it flies.

The fly's compound eyes contain up to 4,000 lenses and it can see danger from every angle.

Once the wings are fully expanded and hardened, the fly will be able to beat them 200 times per second, and tilt them this way and that to make fine adjustments to its flight path.

Retract and recycle
Once the fly is free of its pupal case, the balloonlike ptilium is drawn back into the head by a special set of muscles. Neither the ptilium organ nor the muscles that control it will be needed again, and so they quickly shrink and disappear so that the materials used to build them can be recycled within the fly's body.

The fly's body is covered in sensitive hairs. These can detect tiny movements in the air and allow the fly to feel its way in the dark.

The fly has no chewing muscles and can only take food in liquid form using its spongelike mouthparts. It drools special saliva onto its meals, and uses its feet to mash the food into a soup, which it can then mop up.

Golden-headed lion tamarin

With its magnificent tawny mane, it's easy to see how this South American primate got its scientific name *Leontopithecus*, the lion monkey. Unlike their feline (cat) namesakes, tamarins are tiny and could easily sit in the palm of your hand. In fact, this is a good way to think of this species, whose future is very much in our hands. Nine-tenths of the misty coastal rain forests of Brazil where tamarins live have been cut down, and without intensive conservation the species will become extinct.

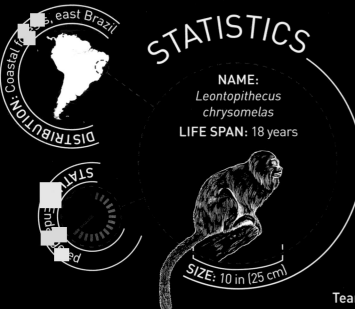

STATISTICS

DISTRIBUTION: Coastal f..s, east Brazil

NAME:
Leontopithecus chrysomelas

LIFE SPAN: 18 years

SIZE: 10 in (25 cm)

The eyes face forward, like our own. This allows the tamarin to judge distance very accurately —an essential skill for an animal that leaps through branches high above the forest floor.

Hanging by their fingernails

Tamarins have clawlike nails at the tips of the fingers to help them cling to the branches and trunks of trees. The middle two fi..rs of each hand are webbed to im.... grip on slippery leaves. But climbing needs practice. Early attempts to return other captive-bred tamarins to the wild ... badly wrong because the released animals weren't used to climbing trees that swayed in the breeze. Some fell to their death. Today's zoo enclosures are much more natural, so captiv.. red tamarins are much better adapted and reintroductions to the wild are more likely to succeed. Now the main problem is finding areas of forest that are safe from loggers.

Team effort

Tamarins live in close-knit family groups of a single breeding male and female, their youngest offspring, and a few older offspring from previous years. With her mate and these other helpers on hand, the female tamarin is one of the few primates capable of raising twins. For most other species of wild primate (monkeys, apes, and lemurs), one baby is more than enough work.

Tamarins have small, sharp teeth used for chopping up fruit and insects, and cutting into trees to release sweet, nutritious sap.

The lustrous fur is kept in condition by regular grooming. Family members groom one another as a way of bonding or reinforcing their relationship.

Great diving beetle

My first encounter with this fierce aquatic predator was as a curious ten-year old. Dabbling in a stream on vacation, I spotted an impressive-looking beast lurking under a stone and decided to add it to the collection of tadpoles I had in a bucket. The Great diving beetle nymph had other ideas—as soon as I grabbed its tail, it flipped around and bit me hard. I learned the painful way that this is not a creature to be messed with, and those tadpoles had a lucky escape!

The long, segmented antennae are multisensory. They are sensitive to touch, temperature, and the smell and taste of chemicals in air and water.

The beetle has large, powerful jaws made of chitin. This is an exceptionally tough material which, along with various proteins, also makes up most of the rest of the exoskeleton. The jaws can easily bite through or crush the bodies of most other freshwater insects, tadpoles, and even small fish.

In addition to its formidable jaws, the great diving beetle has two pairs of palps, used to feel and taste food before it is eaten.

The large compound eyes see well in both air and water.

Young and old
At first glance the young diving beetle, or nymph, looks nothing like its parent. But both have a segmented body, long powerful legs, and those deadly mouthparts.

Life cycle
Great diving beetle nymphs shed their exoskeleton periodically and grow to a maximum length of about 2½ in (6 cm) over about two months. Then they crawl from the water and hide themselves in mud at the water's edge, where they pupate and emerge as winged adults early in the spring. After mating, the female deposits her eggs in slits cut into the stems of water plants.

Sharp spines on the leg joints deter predators such as carp and large frogs, but they are no match for the daggerlike bill of a heron, one of the beetle's few natural enemies.

The beetle breathes air, which it carries in a bubble under its wing cases like an aqualung. Over time, the bubble shrinks and if the beetle is swimming actively it will need to visit the surface every few minutes in order to replenish its supplies of oxygen.

The back legs are slightly flattened and fringed with stiff bristles. They make highly efficient oars, which the beetle uses to row itself rapidly through the water. Here, the back feet are seen thrusting against the water's surface, stabilizing the insect's position.

With adult great diving beetles, telling the sexes apart is easy. In females, the elytra, or wingcases, are grooved along their length, whereas those of males are smooth like this one.

Taking to the air

The adult diving beetle flies just as well as it swims, and after emerging from the pupa it may move from pond to pond in search of a mate or a suitable breeding site. The beetles are sometimes attracted to lights at night and may land on wet roads, greenhouses, or other shiny surfaces, presumably mistaking them for water.

The front legs of this male beetle are equipped with suction pads, which it uses for gripping a female's body when mating.

As in other beetles, the foot, or tarsus, appears to be made up of five segments, although a single muscle runs through, linking them all. The foot ends with two curved claws, which can find grip on most natural surfaces.

STATISTICS

DISTRIBUTION: Europe and Nothern Asia

STATUS: Not threatened

NAME:
Dytiscus marginalis
LIFE SPAN: About 1 year

SIZE: 1½ in (35 mm)

Dragon-headed cricket

With his bulging blue eyes and florid pink face, this crazy cricket looks like an old lady wearing too much makeup. The species is still relatively little known, but this male thrived in a tank in my studio, eating bananas and often serenading me with his deafening mating call. Unfortunately, to human ears, his high-pitched rasping songs are about as romantic as a burglar alarm! He produces the sound by rubbing his wing bases together in a process called stridulation.

STATISTICS

DISTRIBUTION: Borneo

STATUS: Unknown

NAME:
Eumegalodon blanchardi

LIFE SPAN:
A few months

SIZE: 4 in (10 cm)

Step by step

Unlike true grasshoppers, which move around mainly by hopping, this cricket habitually moves with a more sedate walk. Zoologists refer to hopping animals, from frogs and grasshoppers to kangaroos, as saltatorial, and walkers as gressorial. Saltatorial animals are usually easy to recognize by their extra-long hind legs.

Thorny spines on the legs are a deterrent to would-be predators—the cricket would make an awkward and uncomfortable mouthful.

The cricket hears through paired holes at the top of the third leg segment, or tibia, Each opening leads to a membrane, the tympanum, which detects vibrations in the ear in much the same way as an ear drum.

Even strides

This species is set apart from true grasshoppers by having back legs not much larger than other pairs. It can jump when it needs to get out of trouble, but may have to use its wings as well to make a convincing getaway.

Great unknowns

This charismatic animal is just one of thousands of insects about which scientists still know very little. At least it has a name and we know what it looks like. There are more than one million known species of insect, but amazingly, there are probably at least as many again out there still waiting to be discovered—doing so will keep future explorers and entomologists (insect experts) busy for a long time to come.

The cricket's head is protected by a helmetlike case made of fused chitin plates.

Crests of spines run up the back of the head, earning the species its alternative common names of Spiny grasshopper and Spiny devil cricket.

The dark pseudopupils that appear to follow an observer around are an optical illusion. In fact, the cricket is looking in all directions at once.

Close up, the mandibles (jaws) look like the hydraulic tools used by rescue teams to rip open crashed cars. The cricket uses them to chop up its food and in threatening displays.

Long-distance love song

Drago-headed crickets are highly territorial. Males in particular are aggressive toward one another and cannot be kept in the same enclosure. The unusually loud mating call carries a long distance and will reach the ears of females occupying territories some distance away. Females that are ready to breed will respond, and the male will visit them to mate.

Lionfish lurking

The lionfish is an invisible menace to small fish and other unwary visitors to the weedy, sun-dappled waters of shallow Hawaiian reefs. This covert predator loiters in corners, its frills and fringes helping it blend imperceptibly with its surroundings. For incautious prey, the first sign of danger is a surge of water as the lionfish lurches forward, by which time it's often far too late to escape its snapping jaws. For humans, paddling barefoot can be dangerous—the lionfish has fin spines that double as defensive weapons, delivering an excruciatingly painful sting.

The spiny fins serve in self defense. Each spines is modified into a hypodermic needle that pierces the skin of any animal unlucky enough to make contact, delivering a potent venom.

Sting in the name
The end of the lionfish's scientific name is *sphex*, Greek for "wasp," because of its sting. The species is also known as the Hawaiian scorpionfish, a name that carries a similar warning. A third name, turkeyfish, refers to the elaborate featherlike crest.

The large eyes indicate that the lionfish is a visual hunter. The eyes are disguised by a vertical stripe and a growth of tentacles above, which mimics encrusting algae and helps break up the outline of the head.

The lionfish does not use its venom to hunt. Instead, it relies on its superb camouflage to ambush smaller fish. Attacks happen at lightning speed. The huge mouth is fringed with sensory tentacles and lined with small, sharp teeth.

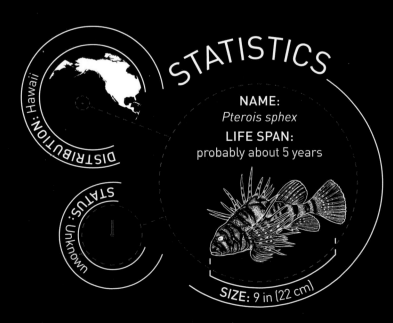

STATISTICS

DISTRIBUTION: Hawaii

STATUS: Unknown

NAME:
Pterois sphex
LIFE SPAN:
probably about 5 years

SIZE: 9 in (22 cm)

Dangerous relative
A close relative of the Hawaiian lionfish, the Indopacific estuarine stonefish *Synanceia horrida*, has the distinction of being the world's most venomous fish. People suffering form stonefish stings may die within hours.

The fanlike pectoral fins may be used to help corner prey—blocking escape routes and driving it back within range of the jaws.

Glossary

ABDOMEN In insects, the rearmost of the three sections of the central body. In vertebrates, the part of the body also known as the belly, containing the stomach and bowels.

ADAPTATION A process of evolution by which organisms become better suited to their environment or lifestyle. Also, a feature produced by this process.

AMPHIBIAN A vertebrate animal belonging to the class Amphibia. Amphibians start life in water as larvae (often called tadpoles), but as adults they breathe air and live at least partly on land.

ANTENNA Also called a feeler, one of a pair of mobile sense organs on the head of insects, crustaceans, and other arthropods. (Plural antennae.)

APPENDAGE A protruding body part, often the jointed legs, antennae, or mouthparts of an arthropod.

ARACHNID Spiders, scorpions, and other animals from the arthropod class Arachnida. Arachnids have four pairs of walking legs and feeding appendages called pedipalps and chelicerae.

ARTERY A blood vessel carrying blood from the heart to other parts of the body.

ARTHROPOD An invertebrate animal such as a fly or a crab, belonging to the phylum Arthropoda, with a segmented body, jointed legs, and an exoskeleton (external skeleton).

BLOOD VESSEL A tube in which blood circulates around the body of animals. There are three types—relatively large arteries and veins, and very fine capillaries.

BROOD To take care of eggs until they hatch. Also, all of an animal's young born and raised at the same time.

CAMOUFLAGE A disguise that helps an animal to blend in with its surroundings.

CARAPACE The hard case covering the upper body of various animals, including some insects and crustaceans.

CARNIVORE Any animal that specializes in eating meat.

CELL The smallest unit of living matter, consisting of a nucleus surrounded by cytoplasm and bound by a membrane. Cells are the building blocks of life.

CHITIN This tough structural carbohydrate is the main material in the outer covering (exoskeleton) of many insects, crustaceans, and other arthropods.

CHORDATE An animal belonging to the phylum Chordata. A chordate's body is supported at some stage in its life by a stiff rod called the notochord. Most chordates are also vertebrates.

CIRCULATION The flow of vital substances, particularly blood, around an animal's body.

CNIDARIAN An animal of the phylum Cnidaria, which includes jellyfish and corals. Cnidarians are very simple, aquatic (water-dwelling) animals with stinging cells and tentacles around their mouth.

COLONY A group of animals living closely together, often relying on one another.

COMPOUND EYE An eye made up of many small lens units (ommatidia), as found in many arthropods.

CONSERVATION The protection and preservation of nature.

COURTSHIP A behavior aimed at encouraging mating—by dancing, singing, presenting food, or otherwise showing off.

CRUSTACEAN A member of the arthropod subphylum Crustacea, which includes animals such as woodlice, crabs, and shrimps. Most crustaceans are aquatic (water-dwelling) and have a hard carapace. They also have two pairs of antennae.

CUTICLE The outermost layer of an organism's covering, made of substances produced by the cells, such as waxes that make it shiny.

DIGESTION The breakdown of food into small particles that can be absorbed and used by an animal's body.

ECHINODERM A member of the phylum Echinodermata. This group of spiny-skinned marine (sea-dwelling) invertebrates includes sea urchins and starfish.

ECHOLOCATION The detection of objects by listening for reflected sound waves, or echoes. It is used by bats and dolphins.

ECTOTHERMIC An ectothermic animal's body heats up and cools down with its surroundings. Reptiles, amphibians, fish, and invertebrates are ectothermic. The opposite word is endothermic (see *warm-blooded*).

EGG A reproductive cell produced by female animals, which combines with a male sperm to produce a new individual. Also, in some animals, a tough-shelled capsule in which the young develops before hatching.

ELYTRA The front pair of wings of some insects, including beetles, which together form a hard case that protects the more delicate second pair of wings used for flying. (Singular elytron.)

ENVIRONMENT The surroundings and conditions in which an organism lives.

EVOLUTION The process by which living organisms change over millions of years.

EXOSKELETON The external skeleton that covers, supports, and protects some invertebrates, especially arthropods.

EXTINCT Having died out, completely and permanently. An extinct species has no living individuals and is gone for good.

FERTILIZATION The joining of male and female reproductive cells (in animals, the sperm and egg) to create a new individual.

FREQUENCY A measurement of sound waves in which higher frequencies sound higher pitched. For example, a squeak is a high-frequency sound compared to a boom.

GENETIC Related to genes and inheritance. Genes are the instructions in cells that control how living organisms develop and function. Animals resemble their parents because they inherit their genes.

GILL An organ used by fish and other aquatic animals to get oxygen from water.

GLAND An organ that produces and releases certain chemicals, such as hormones, milk, or sweat.

GROOMING Cleaning and looking afer the skin, feathers, or fur.

GRUB The young of various insects, also known as a caterpillar, larva, or maggot.

HABITAT The natural home of an animal or plant.

INSTAR One of several early stages in the life cycle of arthropods, between molts.

INVERTEBRATE An animal without a backbone, or vertebral column.

IRIDESCENCE An oily, rainbow-colored shine.

KERATIN A tough structural protein found in hair, feathers, scales, claws, and horns.

LARVA A young stage of an animal that looks different from the adult. Caterpillars, grubs, maggots, nymphs, planulae, and tadpoles are all larvae (plural).

MAGGOT The legless larva of a fly.

MAMMAL An animal belonging to the vertebrate class Mammalia. Mammals are warm-blooded and hairy, and feed their young on milk from glands in the female.

MANDIBLE The paired mouthparts or jaws of an arthropod, often working like pincers.

METAMORPHOSIS The transformation of young forms of certain animals into their very different adult shape—for example, tadpole to frog, or caterpillar to moth.

MIGRATION The regular, often yearly return journey that an animal makes in search of feeding areas or breeding sites.

MIMIC To resemble something, such as a twig or leaf, which helps camouflage, or to resemble a fierce or poisonous animal, which helps self-defense.

MOLLUSK An invertebrate animal belonging to the phylum Mollusca. Mollusks have a soft, muscular body and often a hard shell. Snails, clams, slugs, and squid are all examples of mollusks.

MOLT In arthropods, shedding the entire exoskeleton to allow growth. In vertebrates, shedding skin, hair, or plumage, so that it can regrow. Mammals and birds molt to keep in good condition, to adjust to the weather, or to get ready to breed.

MORPH A variant of a plant or animal species, for example with a distinctive color or plumage pattern.

A beetle's jointed legs and hard casing show that it is an *arthropod*.

This fly's *compound eyes* are made up of hundreds of lenses.

With its armory of stinging cells, the jellyfish is a *cnidarian*.

The Slender loris is a *nocturnal* animal.

NERVE A fiber that sends rapid signals around an animal's body, usually to and from the brain if the animal has one.

NOCTURNAL Active by night. (The opposite is diurnal, or active by day.)

NURSERY The area where young animals are raised.

NYMPH In some insects, a larval stage that resembles the adult and therefore undergoes only partial metamorphosis, without a pupal stage.

ORAL Relating to the mouth.

ORGAN A structure in the body, made of several kinds of tissue, that performs a specific task. For example, the heart is made of muscle and nerve tissue, and has the task of pumping blood around the body.

ORGANISM A living thing, such as an animal, a plant, a fungus, or a bacterium.

OXYGEN A gas found in the atmosphere and dissolved in water. It is taken in by living organisms for use in respiration.

PALP One of the paired, mobile, jointed appendages next to the mouth of an insect, used for feeling, tasting, and handling food.

PARASITE An organism that lives on or in another (the host), from which it gets nourishment or shelter. The parasite benefits, but the host suffers harm.

PEDIPALP One of the pair of leglike appendages near the mouth of a spider or scorpion, used for sensing and handling food, for attacking prey, or in mating.

PEST An animal that causes a nuisance to humans, for example, by attacking crops and livestock, or by spreading disease.

PHEROMONE A chemical released by one animal to communicate with another—for example, to mark a trail, warn off rivals or intruders, or attract a mate.

PHYLUM The highest-level grouping in the classification of the animal kingdom. A phylum, such as Arthropoda, is subdivided into class, order, family, genus, and species in turn. (Plural phyla.)

PIGMENT A chemical substance that produces a strong color.

PITCH The quality of sound given by the frequency of sound waves. High-pitched sounds are squeaky or whining. Low-pitched ones are deep, bass, or booming.

PLANKTON Tiny organisms, often microscopic, including algae and the larvae of invertebrates and fish, which drift in lake and ocean currents.

PLUMAGE The feathers covering a bird.

POPULATION The members of a species that live in a particular place. Also, the total number of individuals of a species worldwide.

PREDATOR An animal that hunts and kills other animals (prey) for food.

PREHENSILE Able to coil around an object and grip it. The tail of a seahorse or a chameleon, for example, is prehensile.

PREY An animal that is killed and eaten by another (a predator).

PRIMATE A mammal belonging to the class Primates, which includes lorises, monkeys, and apes (including humans). All primates have forward-facing eyes and grasping hands.

PROTEIN One of a large class of chemicals containing carbon and nitrogen and made in the bodies of living organisms. Some proteins take part in vital chemical processes in the body and others form body tissues, such as hair and muscle.

PSEUDOPUPIL The illusion of a pupil-like spot in the compound eye of some insects.

PUPA The intermediate, usually immobile stage in the life cycle of some insects, during which the larva metamorphoses into an adult. Also known as a chrysalis. When a larva enters the pupal stage, it is said to pupate.

PUPIL The dark circular or slitlike hole at the front of an animal's eye that controls the amount of light entering by widening and narrowing.

RECEPTOR A cell or group of cells that senses and responds to inputs from the environment, such as touch, heat, light, sound, or chemicals. Receptors occur in the skin and in sense organs, such as eyes and ears.

REPRODUCTION The process of producing young. Reproduction can be sexual (involving mating and the mixing of genes from two parents) or asexual (without mating or mixing).

REPTILE A vertebrate animal belonging to the class Reptilia. Reptiles are ectothermic with scaly skin and include snakes, lizards, tortoises, and crocodiles.

RESPIRATION Breathing—taking in oxygen and getting rid of carbon dioxide, the waste product of respiration. Also, the chemical reactions taking place in every living cell that break down food molecules, with the help of oxygen, to release energy for all of the body processes.

RETINA A light-sensitive layer at the back of the eye, where receptor cells collect visual information and send it to the brain along the optic nerve.

RODENT A gerbil, squirrel, mouse, or other mammal in the order Rodentia, with front teeth specialized for gnawing.

ROOST To rest, usually above ground level, for example, in a tree. Also, a perch or site used by groups of animals for roosting.

SALIVA A liquid produced by glands in the mouth that aids chewing and swallowing. Saliva contains chemicals that begin digestion. In some animals, it also contains toxins that kill or immobilize prey.

SCENT A distinctive smell, often produced by an animal or plant as an advertisement.

SEGMENT One of a series of repeating units in the body of segmented animals such as arthropods and annelid worms.

SKELETON A framework of bones or other hard parts supporting the body of an animal and providing attachment points for muscles. (See also *exoskeleton*.)

SKULL The fused head bones that protect the brain of a vertebrate animal.

SPAWN The eggs of aquatic animals. Also, the act of releasing the eggs.

SPECIES The basic unit of classification of living organisms. Members of a species look like one another and can reproduce by pairing with one another, but not with members of other species.

SPERM A male's reproductive cell, which seeks and fuses with a female's egg cell to fertilize it.

SPIRACLE A small opening in the body of arthropod animals, through which oxygen can pass in and out of the body.

TADPOLE The aquatic (water-dwelling) larval stage of amphibians, particularly frogs and toads. Tadpoles metamorphose gradually into air-breathing adults.

TENTACLE A thin, trailing, or prehensile appendage, often used for hunting.

TERRITORY The part of an animal's habitat that it defends from rival animals, usually of its own species.

THORAX In four-limbed vertebrates, the part of the body between the neck and abdomen, sometimes called the chest. In arthropods, the central body part bearing the walking legs and wings if present.

TOXIN A poisonous substance. Toxins produced by animals are usually proteins.

ULTRASOUND Sound too high in pitch for humans to hear, but heard by many animals. Echolocation calls are ultrasonic.

ULTRAVIOLET Light with a wavelength just less than that of visible blue light. It can be seen by certain animals, but not humans.

URINE A fluid containing toxic waste products from an animal's chemical processes. It is produced by the kidneys and removed from the body by urination.

VEIN A type of blood vessel that carries blood from the body to the heart.

VENOM A toxin produced by an animal to be injected into another by a bite or sting and used for hunting or self defense.

VERTEBRATE An animal with a backbone (vertebral column), made of vertebrae.

WARM-BLOODED A warm-blooded, or endothermic, animal keeps its body constantly warm with internal chemical reactions, no matter whether its surroundings are hot or cold. All mammals and birds are warm-blooded.

ZOOLOGIST A scientist who specializes in the study of animals.

A male Gouldian finch's vibrant *plumage* shows females he is healthy.

A chameleon uses its *prehensile* tail to grip twigs while climbing.

This caterpillar's body is made up of repeating *segments*.

To defend itself, a scorpion injects *venom* with the sting on its tail.

Index

Acknowledgments

Dorling Kindersley would like to thank
Laurie Sherwood and the keepers at
ZSL for facilitating Igor's zoo shoot;
Rob Houston, Claire Nottage, and
Lisa Stock for editorial assistance;
David Ball for design assistance;
Hilary Bird for the index; Margaret
Parrish for Americanization.

The publisher would like to thank the
following for their kind permission to
reproduce their photographs:

(Key: a-above; b-below/bottom;
c-center; f-far; l-left; r-right; t-top)

DK Images: Zoological Society of
London 2cl, 3fcl, 6c, 7tl, 8bl, 8cl, 9bc, 9c,
14-15, 20-21, 36-37, 40-41, 44-45, 45bc,
86-87, 94fbr. **Science Photo Library:**
Patrick Lynch 9tr. **Igor Siwanowicz:** 1cr,
1fcl, 1fcr, 2cr, 2fcl, 2fcr, 3cl, 3cr, 3fcl,
5clb, 5fclb, 6bl, 7b, 7tr, 8bc, 8br, 9bl, 9cr,
10bl, 10br, 10cr, 10-11, 11br, 11c, 12-13,
16-17, 18-19, 22tl, 22-23, 26-27, 27tl,

27tr, 28-29, 29cr, 30-31, 34-35, 38-39,
42-43, 46-47, 48-49, 50-51, 52bl, 52-53,
54-55, 58-59, 59br, 60-61, 62-63, 64-65,
66-67, 68-69, 72-73, 73br, 73cr, 73tr, 74-
75, 76-77, 78-79, 80-81, 82-83, 84bc,
84bl, 84-85, 88bl, 88-89, 90clb, 90-91,
94bl, 94br, 94fbl, 95bl, 95br, 95fbr, 96br.
Anna and Jakub Urbanski: 11tr.

All other images © Dorling Kindersley
For further information see:
www.dkimages.com

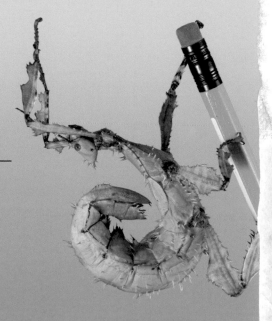

**Giant prickly
phasmid**